ALSO BY ALVIN M. JOSEPHY, JR.

The Patriot Chiefs: A Chronicle of American Indian Resistance

The Nez Perce Indians and the Opening of the Northwest

The Indian Heritage of America

Red Power

The Long and the Short and the Tall

The Artist Was a Young Man

Black Hills—White Sky

On the Hill

Now That the Buffalo's Gone

The Civil War in the American West

America in 1492 (editor)

500 Nations: A History of North American Indians

A Walk Toward Oregon

LEWIS AND CLARK THROUGH INDIAN EYES

Lewis and Clark
Through Indian Eyes

EDITED BY

ALVIN M. JOSEPHY, JR.

WITH MARC JAFFE

ALFRED A. KNOPF   NEW YORK · 2006

THIS IS A BORZOI BOOK PUBLISHED BY ALFRED A. KNOPF

Copyright © 2006 by Alvin M. Josephy, Jr.

www.aaknopf.com

Library of Congress Cataloging-in-Publication Data

Lewis and Clark through Indian eyes / edited by Alvin M. Josephy, Jr.; with Marc Jaffe.—1st ed.

p. cm.

ISBN 1-4000-4267-4

1. Lewis and Clark Expedition (1804–1806)   2. Indians of North America—West (U.S.)—Historiography.   3. Frontier and pioneer life—West (U.S.)—Historiography.
4. Lewis, Meriwether, 1774–1809—Relations with Indians.   5. Clark, William, 1770–1838—Relations with Indians.   6. Lewis, Meriwether, 1774–1809. History of the expedition under the command of Captains Lewis and Clark.   I. Josephy, Alvin M., 1915–   II. Jaffe, Marc.

F592.4 2006

978'.0072'2—dc22   2005049441

Printed in the United States of America
Published April 17, 2006
Second Printing, June 2006

CONTENTS

PART TWO

MANDAN AND HIDATSA OF THE UPPER MISSOURI

WE YA OO YET SOYAPO

THE CEREMONY AT NE-AH-COXIE

THE VOICES OF ENCOUNTER

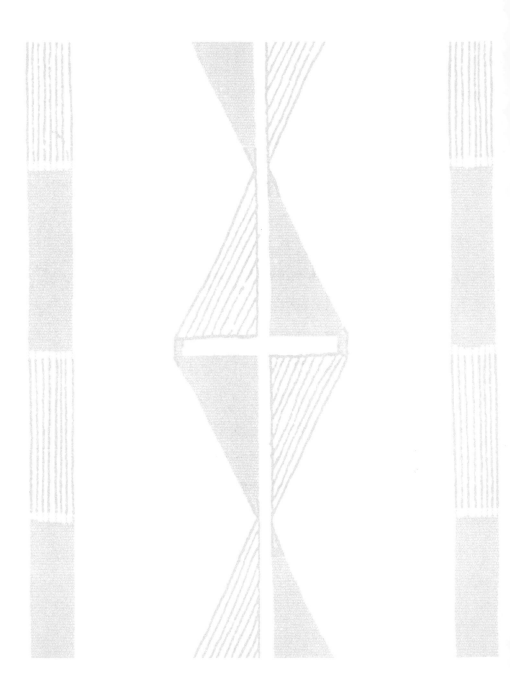

Author's Note

The idea for this book began to take form decades ago in the course of research for my book, *The Nez Perce Indians and the Opening of the Northwest*. It rapidly became clear that the voice of the Indians themselves was not sufficiently heard either in the scholarship or in the published writing about the history of the West. Not much has changed in the years since, which became abundantly clear as we approached the two hundredth anniversary of that undisputed major epic, Lewis and Clark's journey up the Missouri and across the Rockies to the shores of the Pacific. Once again, the Indian voice was virtually unheard in popular historical narrative, journalism, and even film treatments of the event. In 2003, with no full-fledged work by an Indian historian on the Lewis and Clark story in prospect at the time, these nine essays were commissioned over a period of months, resulting in a completed collection early in 2005.

There are many people whom I wish to thank for their invaluable help in bringing about a successful conclusion. First, my thanks to many Indian friends and colleagues, whose suggestions, ideas, and support over many years has been of inestimable help. I also wish to thank my immediate family: my daughters Diane Josephy Peavey, Allison Wolowitz, and Katherine Josephy; my son, Alvin; and my cousin Wendy Cooper for their encouragement and advice, especially during the past two difficult years. Thanks also to Rich Wandschneider of Joseph, Oregon, the executive director of Fishtrap, who was an early, energetic, and creative supporter of the project. And thanks to Ann Close, my editor at Knopf, for her sensitive editorial hand, and to her assistant, Millicent Bennett, for her patient shepherding, especially in the final stages of the publishing process.

And last, my thanks, without reservation, to Marc Jaffe, for his constant companionship in a very involved effort of editorial coordination, from the very beginning to this date—July 2005.

ALVIN M. JOSEPHY, JR.

JOSEPH, OREGON

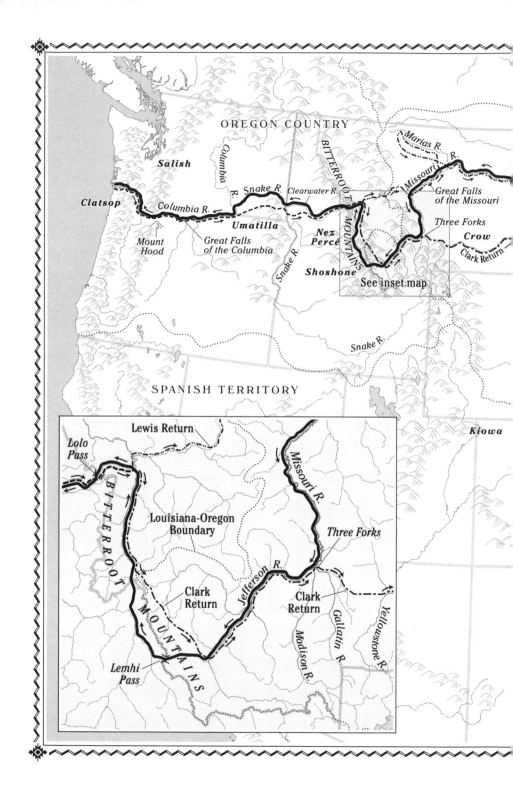

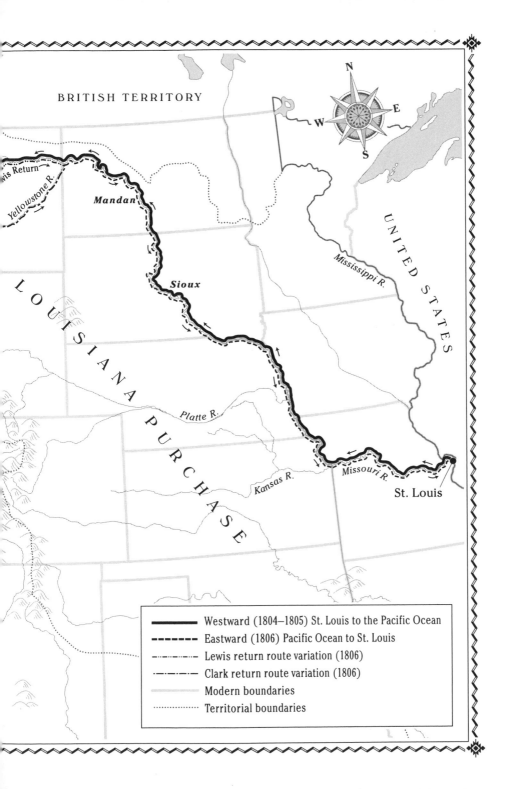

BRITISH TERRITORY

UNITED STATES

Lewis Return

Yellowstone R.

Mandan

Sioux

Mississippi R.

L O U I S I A N A   P U R C H A S E

Platte R.

Kansas R.

Missouri R.

St. Louis

N
W   E
S

—— Westward (1804–1805) St. Louis to the Pacific Ocean
----- Eastward (1806) Pacific Ocean to St. Louis
—··— Lewis return route variation (1806)
—·—· Clark return route variation (1806)
—— Modern boundaries
········· Territorial boundaries

INTRODUCTION

The year 2003 marked the launch of a series of events commemorating the two hundredth anniversary of the journey of Meriwether Lewis and William Clark and their carefully selected adventurers, called the Corps of Discovery. These events were planned, and were to be executed, under the direction of scores of national, regional, state, and local groups that included Indian and non-Indian political figures, historians, National Park Service officials, and others. Coincident with, and to some extent caused by, all this activity, there was a surge of interest in the Lewis and Clark expedition, both in the media and among the general public. Books, documentary films, newspaper and magazine articles across the country, all shed fresh light on the Corps and its accomplishments. Once more, Meriwether Lewis and William Clark were hailed as the engineers of a major, perhaps THE major American epic. *The Journals of Lewis and Clark*, long aborning and finally published in full only in 1904, now attracted new attention and readership. The expedition was truly a remarkable historical episode, and the *Journals* remain a crucial document in American historiography, certainly the most important in the history of the American West.

Both the journey and its leaders' narrative, *The Journals of Lewis and Clark*, justify the enormous amount of attention from writers and historians over the intervening two centuries. In all that time, though, a significant gap existed, which has never been adequately filled. The voice of the Indians themselves has not often been heard. The Indian role in the entire venture, from Jefferson's original instructions to Lewis and Clark to the incalculable importance of native peoples to the success of the journey to historical developments in the decades following, has been fully described and interpreted, but almost exclusively from a white point of view. This book attempts to enrich and broaden the accepted approaches to the telling of a great American story.

There may have been a historical inevitability to the exploration of the American West, but Thomas Jefferson did nothing to slow it down. On January 18, 1803, the president sent the U.S. Congress a secret message containing a request for an appropriation of funds to support an expedition to explore the Missouri River to its source, and thence by land, or water routes as opportunity arose, to the Pacific coast. Although Jefferson had long desired to initiate such an exploration, he could not, at that time, have foreseen its full significance. It was not until June of that year that the amazing news of what we now call the Louisiana Purchase became known in Washington. In any event, the prompt approval of Jefferson's request made possible the organizing of the expedition.

The command of the venture was given to Meriwether Lewis, the president's private secretary, who then selected as co-leader William Clark, another veteran of border military campaigns and the challenges of life in the wilderness. Jefferson gave the two men a clear and simple mission: "to explore the Missouri River, & such principal stream of it, as, by it's course & communication with the waters of the Pacific Ocean, may offer the most direct & practicable water communication across this continent, for the purpose of commerce." A major element in the accomplishment of this mission was to learn as much as possible about the life and culture of the Indians who lived along the route, most of whom, by no coincidence, were crucial to the success of the fur trade, the principal "commerce" to which the president referred.

The Corps of Discovery set out from St. Louis, Missouri, in May 1804, their goal, as directed, to reach the Columbia River and the Pacific Ocean by the most practicable means. The two leaders had spent arduous months in preparation for the journey. Following intensive self-education, particularly on Lewis's part, they engaged a mixed group of military volunteers and experienced men of the border country. With great care they also provisioned their three boats, a fifty-five-foot keelboat and two pirogues, which were to take them up the navigable portions of the Missouri. In addition to the usual powder and shot, cooking utensils and tools, flour and salt, there was "Indian ink" and the blank leather-bound journals that were to be used to record the detailed information required per President Jefferson's instructions. Equally important was the assortment of gifts—medals, needles, mirrors, ribbons, even sheet metal— intended to ease the way in the leaders' negotiations with their Indian counterparts. The Corps numbered forty-eight men in total at the time, with interpreters joining along the way. One of these, George Drewyer (or Drouillard), has been described as the most capable frontiersman in the party; the other, Toussaint Charbonneau, brought with him one of his wives, Sacagawea, who was some six months pregnant. Also included in the party (perhaps not surprisingly, considering Clark's southern heritage) was his personal servant, the black slave York, about whom much has been written. Two points worth noting: the Corps was organized (and disciplined on occasion, as it turned out) very much along military lines. The two captains were supported by sergeants and corporals leading a detachment of privates. Perhaps as a result of such organization, there was only a single fatality during the two-year-long expedition, and that from an unforeseen medical emergency rather than accident or conflict with unfriendly Indians.

The first leg of the journey, through the summer and into the fall of 1804, took the Corps up the Missouri River, north of what is now Bismarck, North Dakota, to winter among the Mandan and Hidatsa Indians. The goal of reaching the Mandans had very likely been established as the expedition began, in the knowledge that the tribes were well settled in their earth-lodge villages, peaceful and familiar with both French and British traders. Farther south along the Missouri, however, the captains had had their first and, as it turned out, their only major confrontation with Indians. A band of the Teton Sioux under Black Buffalo, also familiar with white traders but more aggressive in exacting tribute and exerting control over the river, attempted to block passage. Lewis took a firm stand in resistance, and with the help of diplomacy, a few gifts, and a very small amount of alcohol, the captains were able to persuade the Sioux to back off. The way was open—and stayed that way.

In a log structure called Fort Mandan, built across the river from the main village, the winter passed with the Corps equally well settled and learning to live among the Indians. Lewis and Clark spent much time in planning for the next phase of the expedition, to the headwaters of the Missouri and on to a hoped-for easy crossing of the mountains leading to the river that was to take them on to their ultimate goal. In addition, they prepared a report for President Jefferson on progress thus far, with most attention paid to information about the natives. This latter material gave rise to the famous *Statistical View of the Indian Nations Inhabiting the Territory of Louisiana,* which Jefferson sent to Congress in 1806, perhaps the most important document of its kind and a source of study ever since.

As for the journey to follow, the captains spent most of their time and effort in consultation with members of tribes that came and went at Fort Mandan during the winter. So much so that when the Corps set out in the spring Lewis and Clark had, as Bernard DeVoto says in his classic *The Course of Empire,* "incomparably fuller, clearer and more reliable information about the country ahead of them as far as the Divide than any white men before them had ever had about the West." Early in April 1805, a mixed group of soldiers and engagé boatmen were detached to return to St. Louis in the keelboat, carrying in its cargo the precious and voluminous papers and maps for Jefferson. A much-reduced Corps then set out into what was a white—if not a red—unknown.

By early June Lewis and Clark had reached their next major destination, the Great Falls of the Missouri. While earlier narratives as well as geographical assumptions had suggested that the route across the Rockies from that point on would be relatively painless, the Corps soon discovered that this was not to be the case. There was more than a single range to contend with, and a confusing flow of rivers, north and south, as well as west. Of the several routes available, the captains chose one that proved much longer than that taken on the return trip, but at least it provided a learning experience and a clear view of perhaps the most challenging terrain in the Rocky Mountain West. Guided not only by Sacagawea, but also, even more effectively, by an old man (a Shoshone Indian nicknamed "Toby") and his son, the expedition swung south, then west to the Bitterroot Valley. Then northward along the Bitterroot River, they arrived at the critical westward turning point, Lolo Creek (not far south of present-day Missoula, Montana), leading to the well-marked but horrendously difficult Nez Perce track across the Lolo Pass. There was snow, cold, and hunger, even in September; but by mid-October, having traveled along the Clearwater to the lower reaches of the Snake River, they had come to the beginning of the end of the westward journey, the junction of the Snake and navigable portions of the Columbia, the Great River of the West. If President Jefferson's dream of easy passage across the Rockies was not to be realized, at least the way was cleared by American, not British, claimants for political and commercial dominance in a region not yet part of the United States.

The voyage down the Columbia was fully under way by October 18, with the expedition still facing another difficult passage by canoe and portage through narrow canyons and around falls and rapids until the river widened as it approached the Pacific. Contrary to much of the mythology surrounding Lewis and Clark, those last weeks of travel carried the Corps not through uncharted terrain but along a river that was the heart of heavily populated Indian societies of fishing and foraging peoples, many of whom had had much contact with white traders and sailors.

One could say that the westward exploration ended on December 3, 1805, when William Clark carved his name on a tree along one of the tidal rivers not far from the ocean. Perhaps more important in the reach of history, but still freighted with symbolism, was the building of Fort Clatsop later that month, at the location Clark selected, and named for a small Indian tribe of the area on the southern—the Oregon—side of the Columbia. A Lewis entry in the *Journals,* dated January 1, 1806, reads in part, and perhaps with intended gravity, "our fourtifications being now completed, we issued an order for the more exact and uniform discipline and government of the garrison."

The essays that follow are written by nine Indian contributors—writers, historians, and tribal executives—who were presented with a new Lewis and Clark mission, now two hundred years later, in response to this question: What impact, good or bad, immediate or long-range, did the Indians experience from the Lewis and Clark expedition? Consonant with the mission, the editors made clear that the response to the question would remain in the unfiltered voices of the writers, no matter the theme, tone, or decibel level. Hence the wide variety of style and content. The opening is full of a very contemporary irony, and the other essays in Part One continue to reflect a sensibility conditioned by an Indian experience of today's world, but one still infused by centuries-old tribal traditions both embraced and celebrated. Part Two comprises expressions closer to tribal history and traditions themselves and drawing even more directly on fact and folklore from the past. The closing is poetic and evocative, a summary of an extraordinary historical meeting of races and cultures in what the writer calls "voices of encounter."

ALVIN M. JOSEPHY, JR.
MARC JAFFE
February 2005

PART ONE

FRENCHMEN, BEARS, AND SANDBARS

Vine Deloria, Jr.

VINE DELORIA, JR., was a member of the Standing Rock Sioux Tribe, Fort Yates, North Dakota. He was perhaps the only American whose educational history ranged as far and wide as a New England prep school (Kent), the U.S. Marine Corps Telephone Repair School in San Diego, the Lutheran School of Theology in Chicago, and membership in the faculty of a prestigious state university.

Deloria was a professor of history and an adjunct professor of law, religious studies, and political science at the University of Colorado in Boulder. Best known to the general public as an author (his works include *Custer Died for Your Sins: An Indian Manifesto*, 1969; *Red Earth, White Lies*, 1995; among many other books), he was a college professor from the early 1970s until his death in 2005, and an activist in Indian affairs from the 1960s on. From 1964 to 1967, for example, he was executive director of the National Congress of American Indians; in the mid-seventies he founded and chaired the Institute for the Development of Indian Law; in the nineties, after serving as vice chairman of the Board of the Smithsonian National Museum of the American Indian, he became chairman of its Repatriation Committee.

Vine Deloria, Jr., received honors early and often for his work as a writer and scholar, but unique among these was his nomination in 1974 as one of eleven "Theological Superstars of the Future."

While his Sioux forebears chose confrontation in their encounter with Lewis and Clark, Deloria chose a potent sense of historical irony.

FRENCHMEN, BEARS, AND SANDBARS

Exaggeration of the importance of the expedition of Lewis and Clark is a typical American response to mythology. We prefer our fantasies in opposition to the facts of life. It was a routine venture now revered because we desperately need to have a heroic past, since that pleasure is denied to us in the present. The expedition was initiated following Jefferson's finesse of Congress and the Constitution in the purchase of a mere claim by France that it "owned" a substantial portion of the North American West because a Frenchman had first set foot on lands drained by the Mississippi. Not only did the expedition seek a practical water route to the West Coast with the eventual goal of opening the Pacific to American commerce, but Jefferson also needed to prove that the purchase of an unknown territory was not a white elephant. (He did, however, caution Lewis and Clark to be on the lookout for mammoths while en route.)

Since traditionally historians have understood the journey as the first effort by civilized men to pierce the unknown West, we often tend to clothe the accounts of Lewis and Clark in more heroic terms than they seem to have deserved. Much good history falls by the wayside when we stress the heroics and neglect the context of their journey in our understanding. The expedition actually seems to have been a tedious march from one place to another made known to them by Indians and French traders, with an occasional incident to testify to the strangeness of the land and the unique challenges that the West presented.

After reading through the journals edited by Elliott Coues, my impression of the memorable experiences of the expedition, the things that would have remained with its members years after their return, revolved around three major topics, although I must admit that a strong case might be made for several other themes. But the things that impressed me were the fact that Frenchmen had already explored much of this region so that it was reasonably well known to many people, that there seemed to be an oversupply of bears on the prairies and bottomlands, and that sandbars posed a continuing barrier to the expedition, making the development of a heavy and easy commerce with the Orient via an inland waterway impossible. Indeed, travel later to the Montana area depended heavily on the spring snowmelt and required special flat-bottom boats.

The accounts of the journey to the West Coast contain those wonderful naïve observations that always come with first discovery. Consequently the responses of the Corps of Discovery to these new experiences provide us with good insight into their feelings and what they believed they were doing, and record the occasional misfortunes of the group, which became traumas because they were unexpected. Entries on the return trip record fewer surprises and illustrate the confidence and sometimes arrogance that experience often brings.

That they had the confidence that they could split the little company and explore different river systems with the expectation that they knew the land so well that they could meet again in more familiar territory suggests that they felt they had conquered the West. The final report would therefore be couched in the optimistic terms of men who had overcome severe hardships and now stood ready for another challenge. They had breached the unknown, albeit with considerable assistance from the local inhabitants, and now believed in their own superiority, a mood that would shortly energize people to emulate their feats and bring about the ruination of the Great American West.

Before we examine the Indian understanding of the expedition, let us walk with the explorers on their first encounter with the land and its peoples. We have traditionally been taught to believe that the Lewis and Clark expedition was the first penetration of white men into the western lands. This belief is totally unfounded. The locations of the Mandan villages, scattered from the present North Dakota–South Dakota line along the Missouri River to some distance above present-day Bismarck, were already common knowledge.

Mih-Tutta-Hang-Kusch, a Mandan village. *Painting by Karl Bodmer.*
Courtesy of Joslyn Art Museum, Omaha, Nebraska.

French and British traders had already established a thriving commerce with these villages and the sedentary Indians were accustomed to dealing with foreigners.

A good portion of the trip while moving through wild and unoccupied country did not involve discovery of the West but merely followed paths already well established. Thus when the expedition
visited the Yankton Sioux camp, the Indians were flying a Spanish
flag, and it is well known that these Sioux had attended the British
conference at Albany prior to the American Revolution. They would
also send warriors to support the British during the War of 1812. The
coastal tribes in Washington and Oregon had already been visited by
the English and Spanish and had routed the Spanish expansion.

More important, however, was the presence of French trappers in
the area. The growing population of half-breeds of French-Indian heritage, some people representing second and perhaps even third gen-

erations of men out on the plains, indicated that white men had lived among the tribes for a considerable period of time. Above the great bend near present-day Pierre, South Dakota, the expeditioners visited a Frenchman's house that had no protective palisade, testifying to the fact that the French had successfully melded with the Indians long ago.

French colonial policy had encouraged intermarriage with the Indians and the exchange of children to create kinship bonds with the eastern tribes. The French sought to create a new kind of society of mixed Euro-Indian genetic background that would and could hold the lands claimed by the French king under the Doctrine of Discovery by appealing to their common ancestry. This class of people was now temporarily loyal to whoever could enhance their fortunes. Most of them had extensive experience in wandering the western lands, and, in sharing their knowledge about the land and its people, they enabled Lewis and Clark to anticipate some of the problems that lay ahead. But they had no loyalty to the Americans, nor would they have for some time to come.

The Frenchmen represented a good deal more than easing the psychological burdens of the unknown lying ahead for the expedition. Indeed, their presence indicated the existence of a society in which manufactured goods were becoming increasingly valuable, as steel knives replaced flint weapons and guns were coveted for both hunting and war. The value to be given in exchange for these industrial products would have to be the skins and hides of animals that were temporarily valuable when beaver hats were stylish or when there was a lack of available leather on the European markets. The land could sustain the wildlife it had but was not so productive that animals could replenish their numbers in the face of extensive hunting above and beyond simple human subsistence. The primary objects of Indian commerce were the hides and skins of the animals that also inhabited the land, and there were a finite number of these creatures, although at the time the herds of grazers seemed without number.

Actually in the journals we find few references to large herds of buffalo or even to the massive dams and villages of the beaver, whose pelts would later be the primary items of trapping and trading. Beaver seem to merit sparse attention when recording the fauna of the region. There are probably more references to rattlesnakes than to beaver, since the men seemed almost hypnotized by these serpents, hardly an item of trade. Lewis and Clark almost certainly saw the wildlife as a barrier to be overcome and not as commodities that would constitute the major portion of trade for the next eight decades.

Some of the half-breeds were not descendants of the local tribes. Pierre Dorian, for example, seems to have been part Iowa Indian, as does his wife. Here we see the results of the displacement of tribes in the Midwest who had been trading with the French and British for more than two centuries. Although there had been no removal treaties affecting the midwestern tribes at that time from which these people might have been fleeing, the fabric of their communal life had long since been torn apart by intermarriage and trade wars. As members of the eastern tribes had experienced the course of empire, they joined in and moved west to become a part of the impending invasion and serve as bicultural brokers in the transactions that lay ahead.

This new class of people would also help open the Pacific Northwest to commerce and exploration. As the Hudson's Bay Company extended its trading posts and influence in the western Rockies and Columbia basin, it employed Iroquois voyageurs who had only a smattering knowledge of the Christian religion but loved to sing Catholic hymns, relying on their rhythms to measure the oar strokes of the trade canoes. These hymns would later inspire the Nez Perces and Flatheads to send a delegation to St. Louis in search of these power songs, triggering the missionary movement toward the Oregon country that ended in disaster for all concerned.

Could these people be described as an indigenous population as we think of one today? To the expedition they were indistinguishable from the local tribes except for the obvious language differences and the warlike proclivities of the tribes claiming and defending extensive territories. Certainly they were seen as a different class from tribal Indians in Canada, who eventually become known as the Metis (mixed-blood people), the constituency of Louis Riel, who regarded themselves as equal members of Canadian society. They appear later in the 1870s as invaders of the northern hunting grounds, feared and resisted fiercely by the tribes living in the United States. Annually they brought large numbers of hunters with freight wagons and families south across the border to hunt buffalo when their own herds had been thinned out, thus escalating the depletion of the northern buffalo herd more rapidly than expected.

Certainly the invasive half-breeds played a critical role in arranging the first treaties between the United States and the northern Plains tribes, treaties incidentally negotiated by William Clark after his exploring days were done. As time went on American whites became the scouts, hunters, and interpreters for subsequent expeditions mounted in St. Louis and Leavenworth, and with some exceptions the French-Indian half-breeds declined in importance. Their descendants today dominate tribal politics in most of the Great Lakes and Plains tribes. Indeed, for some tribes, having French ancestors rather than English is a sign of distinction.

Think of what these people represented, however, and we begin to visualize an alternative possible scenario for the settling of the West. The French colonial policy was to encourage intermarriage with the natives and the exchange of children who would be raised in a different society so that over time they would help create a society that treated lands, resources, and people in a much different manner than the English/Americans did. Would the interior of the United States have been developed with a goal of maintaining a sustainable yield of products rather than of exhausting the resources? Would treaties even have been necessary if the various tribes had adopted enough of French culture that they adapted their institutions to resemble those of western Europe and guaranteed equality in both law and custom to new settlers of the region?

Could a mixed-blood government have dealt with the United States on better terms? We would like to think so, although the experiences of the Five Civilized Tribes suggest otherwise. But the Five Tribes possessed valuable farming lands in the South, whereas the northern plains hardly offered the settlers much comfort, so the demand for land would not have been as intense. To what degree would mixed-bloods' willingness to accommodate themselves to technology and opportunity have produced an ecologically sound society?

This distant prospect seems not impossible if we read the journals of the trip. From St. Louis to the Mandan villages it appears that the Frenchmen had a vital place in the region's social environment. Quite casually we learn that the French were building houses and settling in near the Big Bend without any immediate or prolonged conflict with the tribes using the same area as hunting grounds. We can understand the sense of relief felt by the men whenever the expedition came across Frenchmen, as if they had brought the entirety of the European perspective with them. That the Frenchmen felt entirely at home and possessors of the same knowledge of the land as the Indians suggests that in large part the Gallic colonial goal had been achieved.

The experience of the Yankton Sioux with the French and Americans is interesting and demonstrates how deeply the French had intruded into Indian life. As the Corps of Discovery approached the Yankton Sioux territory they encountered Pierre Dorian, Jr., the son of their interpreter who had ensured that they receive a warm and friendly reception. Instead of assuming the haughty attitude they often showed toward Indians, Lewis and Clark's negotiations with the Yanktons went smoothly. Their generosity in giving the chiefs both medals and clothing impressed the Indians. A Yankton chief summarized the difference: "I went formerly to the English, and they gave me some clothes; when I went to the Spanish they gave me a medal. But nothing to keep it from my skin; but now you give me a medal and clothes."

Lewis and Clark seem to be at a disadvantage here. The Yanktons were not inexperienced men. They had already negotiated agreements with the Spanish and English. Before the Corps moved on upriver, a delegation of chiefs was headed downstream to St. Louis to make a treaty with the United States, indicating that American diplomacy had already reached the Missouri River tribes, although no formal treaties would be made until 1815. Lewis and Clark thus confirmed but did not initiate formal relationships with these people. In a moment of diplomatic genius they wrapped the newborn son of a chief, Struck by the Ree, in the American flag, thereby ensuring steadfast loyalty to the United States. The infant lived to be over ninety years of age and always sided with the United States. Even the Yankton half-breeds were loyal to this cause.

In visualizing a possible alternative history, we come to realize that the English version of European culture always represented high institutional barriers within which people were controlled and made to perform certain political rituals. These institutional rules had little meaning unless and until there was sufficient national power to enforce them. Who could be more dangerous to this French-Indian society than the Americans with their wistful effort to duplicate their vague memories of the mother country—England. We see throughout early colonial history the desire to re-create the English way of life in North America, and this hidden motive must certainly underlie the vision of the Lewis and Clark expedition.

New York, New England, New Jersey, Syracuse, Athens, and New Bedford—everywhere we look east of the Mississippi we find the theme repeated. Everywhere we find people trying to duplicate the Old World and, as in a Rambo movie, displaying the attitude of "This time we win," responding to half-remembered memories of European feudalistic oppression. When settlement reached the Great Plains, the experience of the New England settlements, now remembered as a cultural paradise, became the model and changed the image of American civilization. People began to lay out towns in the old New England format of the village green or commons, with settlements in square blocks, the wealthiest inhabiting the center of town and the poor clinging to the outskirts or later living south of the railroad tracks. Where there were an insufficient number of people to use a traditional town pattern, main streets and even corners sought to preserve the image of proper settlement.

Notice that as American settlement moved away from the coastal plain and across the Appalachians, towns, states, and rivers were given Indian names with increasing frequency, indicating a movement away from European nomenclature toward the perspectives of the indigenous peoples. Note also that the permanent settlers were farmers, planting corn, the Indian food, because it was only with great difficulty that wheat seeds could be safely preserved over a winter for the next year's plantings. European plants would come, but much later. Where we once found French accommodation to the people and the land, we now find the American/English practice of appropriation of lands, removal of the indigenous peoples to isolated corners of the land, and the desire to implant a foreign personality upon the region, drawing straight lines in the earth and eliminating everything that came before.

The foremost requirement in maintaining a society is that of mutual respect among its members. Lewis and Clark, from their comments in the journals, had little respect for the Indians or their institutions. They tended to see Indians as scheming to do them evil, and a sense of impending danger colors many of their recorded comments. Yet other people visiting the tribes were not nearly as blind to what they were seeing. Sometime after the expedition, another American, Henry Marie Brackenridge, visited the Arikara villages, and his comments are worth noting: "we here see an independent nation with all the interests and anxieties of the largest; how little would its history differ from that of one of the Grecian states! A war, a treaty, deputations sent and received, warlike excursions, national mourning or rejoicing, and a thousand other particulars, which constitute the chronicle of the most celebrated people."[1]

As noted earlier, one of the most annoying and dangerous obstacles the expedition met was their continuing encounter with bears, now

1. Henry Marie Brackenridge, "The Arikara Villages," in *Exploring the Northern Plains 1804–1876,* ed. Lloyd McFarling (Caxton, Idaho: The Caxton Printers, 1955), 31.

identified as grizzly bears but described as "white bears" in the journals. These creatures were very aggressive and quite territorial—they often pursued members of the expedition vigorously, chasing them up trees on several occasions. In the minds of Western historians, bears usually bring to mind Hugh Glass and his epic crawl across the prairie after being mauled by a mother bear protecting her cubs. Our traditional vision of the western prairies conceives a land filled with impossibly massive herds of grazing animals, primarily buffalo, antelope, and deer. Therefore, to find the land teeming with bears comes as a great surprise to readers.

Actually, the whole continent was overstocked with bears according to early reports. A French missionary at St. Genevieve, the first French settlement on the Mississippi, across the river and a little south of present-day St. Louis, once spent a day relaxing, watching the Mississippi carry its debris south, and counted fifty bears swimming across the river during the daylight hours. James Pattie, an early explorer in the 1830s, counted three hundred bears on the Santa Fe Trail during the course of a day's journey. Estimating fifteen hours of daylight, that's twenty bears an hour, or one every three minutes. These figures should not be passed off as exceptions to the expecta-

Member of the Lewis and Clark expedition up a tree, escaping a grizzly bear.
Courtesy Beinecke Rare Book and Manuscript Library, Yale University.

tion that grazing animals were most numerous. Indeed, considering the scarcity of fruits and berries on the western plains, it would appear that the bears the expedition encountered were less vegetarian than we would like to believe. They must have been one of the most feared predators on the plains, hunting the sick and old animals in the herds of edible game. There is no question that they saw the members of the expedition as food, not friends.

Why this response from grizzlies as the party moved across the land? Did the bears see vulnerability in the white men they could not detect in the Indians? The Indians of all tribes had a long-standing and complex relationship with bears. For many tribes the bear was a prophet, and having a dream about bears would almost certainly endow someone with the power to find lost objects.

Other tribes saw the bear as a medicine animal, after watching him dig for roots that were as useful to humans as they were to the bears.

The Utes, far south of the trail taken by Lewis and Clark, saw the bear as a religious personality and their bear dance reflected the status he enjoyed with them. One of the primary rituals performed by medicine men from the Minnesota woods to the Rockies was called the Bear Walk in which, with the assistance of the bear power, religious leaders could transform their shape from a physical body to a ball of light and travel to distant locations, there to perform feats of good or evil.

In 1841, D. D. Mitchell, who would later negotiate the first treaty at Fort Laramie with the tribes of the northern plains, reported an experience with the Indians of the Missouri River that was so incredible that it challenges our sense of the rational. While visiting one of the Arikara villages, he was invited to a ritual to be performed by the bear-medicine men. People gathered in an earth lodge, and the seven elders sang several songs, said prayers, and then instructed a young man to go out and bring them a certain kind of clay. From this clay they began to mold little figures of men, horses, and buffalo.

When they had finished making the little creatures, they placed them in the center of a large cleared space in the dwelling. Then one of the elders asked the little men if they wanted to hunt, and, receiving an affirmative answer, he gave them permission to do so. Suddenly the little figures began to move, clay men on clay horses chasing clay buffalo that began stampeding and trying to escape. The spectators in the lodge watched in awe as they observed a miniature hunt take place, identical in most respects to their method of hunting the big animals. At the end of the hunt the bear-medicine men told the clay figures to jump into a fire that had been burning inside the lodge. They ran and galloped into the fire where they were hardened and burned. When the fire cooled, the clay figures were taken out of the ashes and smashed beyond recognition. The clay was then returned to the spot from where it had been taken. Mitchell said he couldn't believe his eyes.

This account seems unbelievable, and yet it was not related by Indians seeking prestige but was carefully noted by an experienced frontiersman who would have severely scrutinized the ritual for any sign of fakery. Skeptics may argue that here was a case of mass delusion, that the Indians, being superstitious, would believe anything. But the Indians lived by their wits in a potentially hostile environment and were not easily deluded. They had to be aware of everything in the environment around them to determine if danger from man, beast, or nature was imminent. Would well-developed senses and incisive powers of observation have suddenly abandoned these people and in their place ignorant acceptance of illusions occur? If such a delusion did occur, then the bear powers should be recognized as so powerful they could seize and hypnotize a whole village plus a group of outside observers.

We know that the northern Plains tribes and mountain tribes were spiritually involved with the bear and buffalo. A glance at the names Indians gave themselves will confirm that the bear was much admired and played a prominent role in people's lives. Could the bears have foreseen the coming chaos on the plains represented by the presence of the expedition, when waves of settlers would bring a commercial civilization to what had been an unrestricted commons? While the question may border on the mystical, we do have the fact that the journals record frequent attacks on members of the party. Whereas in much of the other literature on the frontier we find encounters with bears initiated by humans disturbing the animals, who then responded with a defensive posture, in the case of Lewis and Clark, we find aggressive bears that proclaim their mastery of the land, fear nothing, and take steps to repel invaders.

Some mysteries we can never unravel. While they may be easy to understand in one context, they offer little meaning in another. But let us consider a remote, but possible, scenario. The feat performed by the seven bear-medicine men of the Arikaras was an effort to gain the bears' assistance in hunting. Could they not, in another ceremony, have made clay figures of the men of the expedition along with little clay bears and then commanded the little spirits to interfere with the work of the expedition as it traveled west? Such things are not impossible, and we do not know how the Indians felt about the impolite attitude shown by the expedition's members and the rigid application of white men's law when confronted with the need to exchange gifts or locate strayed horses. We do know that Lewis and Clark were unnecessarily harsh to the Indians on these occasions, and there must have been some hard feelings when the expedition left on its westward journey.

We come then to the sandbars. Sandbars are a major topic in almost all literature about the exploration of the West that features rivers. Indeed, Mark Twain went into great detail about changing sandbars on the Mississippi and said that the Missouri was even more treacherous in shifting its debris from one bank to another. Western rivers were impassable during the spring runoff, when they became torrents of water scouring banks and radically changing streambeds. In the summer they were often just isolated pools of water in a dry land. The Platte River at times is merely a small trickle of water moving within large sandbars. When we try to visualize mountain men bringing flatboats loaded with furs from the rendezvous down the Platte, we cannot begin to build a sensible scenario. Could that streambed ever support any kind of boat?

As the expedition moved northward toward the Mandan villages, we find them engaged in the most tedious and backbreaking work to get their flatboat and provisions past the many obstacles in the Missouri River. West of present-day Yankton as the river bends to go due north for a distance, the party found what appeared to be an ancient fort, and they note the dimensions of what they supposed were the ruins of a previous settlement. While later commentators have claimed the location to be merely the result of sandbars changing places, Lewis and Clark measured some straight long lines to the embankment, and reported them sufficiently linked together to give the appearance of a deliberate construction. This observation caused them to regard the site as the result of human endeavors rather than the whimsical deposits of a swollen river. Rivers do not, as a rule, create long straight embankments.

We know from the excavations near Crow Creek, South Dakota, that some rather substantial villages were built on tributary creeks and bends in the Missouri itself. Scholars assume that some unknown disaster hit these villages, whether adjacent enemies or unexpected plagues, causing them to be abandoned. The surviving inhabitants, if any, are seen as taking up the hunting life again when agriculture and intertribal trade were no longer viable occupations. How severe the depopulation was, or when it might have occurred, remains in the province of academic speculation. Could sandbars have made such radical changes in the life of these people that they found the site of their villages untenable in view of the spring floods?

We do know that many of the population centers in North America appear to have suddenly been abandoned—Cahokia, Chaco Canyon, the Ohio mounds, and the Salt River valley settlements. Do the sandbars represent the prehistory of North America in a way that we cannot fathom? Could they be the determining factor in the lives of people we have not yet identified? Today we cannot test any theories in this regard because the Missouri River has been tamed for its hydroelectric potential, and since the dams were built, islands no longer appear. We think we know fairly well the village sites and excavations now covered by the filling of the dams, and they provided some clues to both historic and prehistoric life and occupation. Eliminating the sandbars, then, became the final step in taming the river and the region. But the sandbars will eventually win, just as the region is being depopulated, because the silt will gradually fill in the great dams on the Missouri.

Some Indians seemed to know about the future developments of the region from ancient religious prophecies. Many tribes have traditions that speak of a strange race coming and subduing them. Others speak of visions of buffalo being replaced by a spotted creature that would prosper briefly and then begin to disappear. In the 1870s an old Yankton Sioux medicine man named Red Leaf was on his deathbed at the White Swan Landing on the reservation in southern South Dakota. His relatives comforted him by relating that they had selected a fine strong cottonwood tree near the river for his burial. He mustered his energy and told them he wanted to be buried in the white man's style in a hole in the earth. He drew his bow one last time and sent an arrow far above the river to a knoll that jutted out in the Missouri breaks. "Bury me there," he said, "and dig deep and put many stones on me for I wish to sleep undisturbed." When the Pickstown dam was completed, the waters flooded his former residence at the landing, covering the riverside trees, and came within fifteen feet of Red Leaf's grave.

Having speculated on the Frenchmen, bears, and sandbars, we must ask, within that context, how the Indians responded to the Lewis and Clark expedition. Certainly non-Indians were not a surprise to them, although they did not see very many at any one time, so that the expedition was understood as simply another group, albeit without women and children. Many upriver tribes held this attitude so that chiefs who had visited St. Louis and told about the infinite number of white men were often ridiculed and sometimes killed for lying. That they could guess the immediate meaning of the presence of these explorers is debatable. Instead, they worked them into their daily lives as if they belonged to the web of life already present.

Sending men home as Lewis and Clark did might have been unusual but not a novelty. Hiring Charbonneau and his wife was perhaps the most important decision in western American history, since Sacagawea proved to be the deciding factor between success and failure of the expedition. Her memory was so extraordinary that we often do not understand it. She had traveled as a captive from the Rockies to the Missouri River years before, and this distance is considerable. Yet she remembered the way west, which was actually a reversal of the path she and her captors had originally taken so that hardly any landmark would have been familiar. This kind of memory is peculiar to North American Indians and is a talent far above mere retention of data. Lucien Levy-Bruhl, in his book *How Natives Think*, remarked on what he called topographical memory with a comment worth repeating:

> Among North American Indians this topographical memory is something marvelous; it is quite enough for them to have been in a place only once for them to have an exact image of it in their minds, and one which will never be lost. However vast and untravelled a forest may be, they cross it without losing their way, once they have got their bearings.[2]

History often seems like a ritual drama in which, as Shakespeare noted, we are but poor minor players enacting a predetermined role. In the case of the Lewis and Clark expedition, there was one absolutely essential factor in its success—Sacagawea. Had she belonged to any other tribe, we would be reading an entirely different history today. Mathematically what are the chances that when Lewis and Clark needed a guide she would be available, and what

2. Lucien Levy-Bruhl, *How Natives Think* (London: George Allen & Unwin Ltd., 1926), 112.

are the chances they would encounter her tribe at the time of their severest crisis? What were the chances that Cortez would arrive on the Mexican shores in the year when Quetzalcoatl was expected? What were the chances that Joshua Lawrence Chamberlain would be commanding the Union troops at Little Round Top and choose that exact moment to order his charge? One of the real messages of the Corps of Discovery journey is the possibility that, as history turns on highly improbable circumstances, the important events of our lives may indeed be already mostly predetermined.

Consequently, while Lewis and Clark believed that history was being made, and certainly American history was being made, the Indians felt that their lives would continue as usual. I doubt if any winter counts, the Indian calendars recording the most memorable event of the year, even recorded the arrival of the expedition or their prolonged stay during the winter. It would have taken greater prophetic powers than the Indians possessed or keen contemplation of the consequences of the expedition for the tribes to understand what the exploration would mean. There was no reason to suppose that the game would be hunted to extinction or that they would suffer epidemics and barbaric treatment by others following in the wake of the expedition. These strangers sought only to learn as much as they could about the land, its animals and resources. Why then had they come, and what explained the intensity with which they scoured the land, seeking its secrets? That these thoughts did not cross their minds is one of the great tragedies of the Indian story because later adventurers took the hospitality they offered as a sign of weakness, with deadly consequences to the Indians.

Events would move with amazing rapidity once the expedition returned to St. Louis. The War of 1812 had dire consequences for the tribes along the Missouri. Required by the Treaty of Ghent to restore the Indian allies of each side to a state of peace, the United States took advantage of the pledge and promptly moved far up the Missouri, signing treaties that it claimed recognized their control and sovereignty over the respective tribes.

The freedom with which people could move in the trans-Missouri west after the river path to the great Rocky Mountains was opened encouraged the mountain men to eliminate the middlemen of the fur trade—the tribes—and secure their own fortunes by trapping the beaver. In 1822 the Ashley-Henry venture began the real exploration of the region. When the beaver were trapped out, many of these men became scouts for the army and, knowing the country and people intimately, prepared the way for gold miners, railroads, and eventually the settlers. Immediate commercial returns on goods encouraged people to forsake the river system and use two new trails—to Santa Fe and Oregon—dividing the immense herds of buffalo and forecasting the end of freedom for the Plains tribes.

Although described as the Great American Desert, the plains were finally conquered by technology, most notably the barbed wire that enabled settlers to fence their lands and the railroads that provided a reasonably quick form of transportation for farm and ranch products. Once railroad building began, the frontier disappeared within a generation. Periodic droughts made the plains an unreliable location for a New England–inspired civilization, and during the twentieth century, settlements existed only with some form of subsidy. In this generation the unsettling of the plains has been proceeding at almost the same pace as their once optimistic peopling in the half century before. Strangely the buffalo, once the pariah of the region as the major barrier to full settlement, has been making a dramatic comeback in those very areas where the last herds existed before the near-extinction of the animals.

In the long run of history, the Lewis and Clark expedition may be but a footnote to a destructive cycle that came and went in the western lands. It is significant then that the success of the much admired expedition depended almost exclusively on a lucky break— obtaining Sacagawea as the guide and taking advantage of the

Indians' indelible memory for the land. The memory of the old pre-settlement days still lingers in the villages of the reservations, and as tribes work to secure titles and access to their sacred sites again, the passing of Lewis and Clark will become a minor event in some future rendering of Indian history.

WHAT WE SEE

Debra Magpie Earling

DEBRA MAGPIE EARLING, a member of the Confederated Salish and Kootenai Tribes of Montana, is one of the most accomplished new writers to come out of the American Northwest. She has published fiction and essays in numerous anthologies and journals, including *The Last Best Place, Talking Leaves: An Anthology of Native American Writers, The Best of Northern Lights, Circle of Women, Reinventing the Enemy's Language,* and *Ploughshares.* In 2003 her novel *Perma Red* won the American Book Award, the WILLA award, the Spur Award, and the Mountains and Plains Booksellers Association Award. She lives in Missoula and teaches there at the University of Montana.

Debra Magpie Earling's Salish ancestors warmly welcomed Lewis and Clark in September of 1805. However, as she writes in her essay, "In 1872, just sixty-seven years after Lewis and Clark had arrived in the valley, everything the Bitterroot Salish had held dear would be taken from them."

WHAT WE SEE

Imagine one day, a great wind chases the ghosts of clouds from the sky. Light slants on the river to lift a brutal shimmering spirit of water. And just above the shadowed green currents where the white gnats are furiously circling, a smell is rising that catches in you like sorrow. In the fields, the deer are still, not even their tails are twitching. Dense heat palms the small of your back. No draft from the river cools you. In this moment you stand alone. The day holds the promise of winter kill, huckleberries black and round in the mountains, berries so ripe if the wind stirred you would smell the tar of their scent. In the low fields bears swat the chokecherries from their branches. In this still hour, the earth is offering blessings.

A low sound is buzzing, not the horseflies, not the grasshoppers clicking in the drying grass but a sound that burns in your throat, the warning you do not wish to recognize. Gut fear is the taste of rusted earth you cannot scrape from your mouth. Your grandfather told you there would come a day when a blistering fever would rise from the belly of the river and the people would not survive. But the elders were always talking crazy.

You were young, full of your own battle stories, when your grandfather crouched low in the brittle weeds to tell you the things he thought you should know. His breath was a sour film that hovered between you, his eyes age-whitened and blind. You did not squat down beside him but stayed standing, your eyes straying to the young women bathing in the smoking winter river. He did not shield his face or flinch into the dazzling dry sun. His gaze was calm and sure. You forgave his tears, and shadowed him. You had little patience to hear his stories of death. Sickness was not your enemy. But as the old man told you his story he began to weep like a woman, his shoulders hitching so violently that the young women soon gathered their clothing and hurried past you, ashamed and frightened.

Today his story returns to you. And here is the story he tells you:

Believe in prophecy and vision, he had said, because our people have always understood the language of the land.

We have always known that the river speaks to us, that the pop of shale beneath our feet signals someone has passed the trail before us. Birds tell us when we are too close to their nests. Grass ticks when a rattler is waiting. Stinging nettle perfumes the air when we are too close to dangerous water. Trees rush with the sound of water when there is no wind, their boughs waving fiercely above us, when an enemy is near. If Rabbit appears suddenly and twitches his ears, we know to drop to the ground before lightning sizzles past us. Hummingbird turns red before he enters our lodges to signal a young person will sicken. Rocks soften beneath our feet when we pray. Sun touches the faces of the dead to quicken their journey home.

The land has always carried the vision of prophecy, the old man said.

In your lifetime a sickness will find the people. It will kill your family. Pay attention.

The first sign. You will smell the blood in the throats of the people. Soon after their chests will flush fire hot. Cherry stains will appear on their hands and feet, then blossom on their chests. Before the sun appears again, the stains will ripen to black, then burst. You will never forget the smell of yellow blood. It will stink in your nostrils when you are an old man. The people will weep blood. And because the people will be too sick to pray, they will also be too sick to drag their children's bodies to burial. The sickness will pop and bubble beneath skin, hiss like a thousand snakes. On your face the scars will be as deep as the first joint of my thumb. The scars will sear your body forever. The beautiful women will become ugly. They will hide their faces from their husbands. Their pockmarked faces will frighten the children. They will become witches.

The sickness will destroy everything you love because it carries the power to change people's hearts. Years after the sickness has passed, the people will twitch like hunted deer before their enemies. Because the people have known this sickness they will make their choices based on fear.

A terrible darkness will shadow the people. For a long while they will turn from prayer. Even the wise people of all the Indian nations will lose their ability to reason for a time. The sickness will be so great that men will believe they have lost their power, and they will do terrible things to regain it. In many tribes men will trade their young wives to old men. They will give away things they do not own for useless trinkets. Because the people have known a sickness no medicine can cure they will seek out the others' power. They will trade the great power the animals have given us, and hand their medicine bundles to the people who are coming to destroy us. They won't know there is no power that can save them from their own weakness.

The sickness will come from far away. It is traveling toward us now. The sickness will travel on the backs of men like the ticks that burr on the buffalo.

Sickness is only the first omen, the first sign of the change to come.

Strange men will soon haunt the land. They cannot hide from you and they do not wish to. Their footsteps will sound loudly on the worn paths we have walked. If you happen on them in the forests, you can recognize them for they are white-fleshed and the trees cannot hide them. Do not mistake them for spirits. They are white men, solid in body, as I am. They will come to you in friendship and give the people arrowheads harder than stone, weapons we have never seen. They will cage the birds, the animals. One day they will cage the people. Those they do not cage they will kill. Listen, my grandson, for the day will arrive soon when you will see a rain of small fire before the buffalo roll down in the grasses. And all that will be left of the buffalo will be mountains of bones. The white man is coming. Sickness and death will herald his arrival. Prepare now. They are coming.

My mother has told me that the people have always held prophecies. The Bitterroot Salish knew when the white man would come. They knew his arrival would bring hardships the people have never known. The Salish knew their lands would be stolen, that the people would starve, the valley would flood with settlers. The strangeness of the arrival of Lewis and Clark could not erase the certain knowledge of the people's knowing. Though there is no record I can point to, no physical evidence I can submit as argument that a prophecy existed, I know from the old stories that my people foretold the coming of the white man.

When I was a senior in college I visited Blind Mose in his home that bordered the St. Ignatius Cemetery. He was our old one. His small sand-shingle house sat squat on scuffed dirt like bare bones on the earth. Though he has been dead for many years, his house still rests above the graveyard where he sleeps now. Burdock and pig-weed hide his darkened windows, hollyhocks whisper at his nailed door. Whenever I visit the grave of my great-grandmother, I pass by his house and nod my thanks to him. Like so many good things, he has passed from us.

Blind Mose would speak only Salish, though he could speak English fluently. I have heard people say that he refused to speak English because he didn't accept the white man's ways. When I was in my twenties, I liked the idea that an elder would shun assimilation and refuse to speak the enemy's language. But as I have grown older, I think there are many reasons why he would choose to speak his native tongue exclusively.

Blind Mose never possessed the gift of eyesight, so words for him were as dense and solid as vision. The world for Blind Mose was formed, framed, and defined by the specificity of his mother tongue. Because the tribe depended on the land for survival, place-names had to be exact descriptions of locale. But Blind Mose knew more than place-names. He could describe the scent and touch of wild rye and licorice root, fireweed, and meadow rue, the papery leather scent of horsetail, and the lemon-pine taste of wild-sunflower stems. He knew by sniff the pepper-clean smell of watercress and the spot where it nestled in the shallow stream pools. He knew all these things in the storied detail of the Salish language.

All of the people who were significant in his life had spoken Salish. Almost every recollection of his long life, every important moment of his days, was expressed in his first language. The priests had beaten him when he spoke his language, had drilled him with

English, had seared his head with kerosene. He was punished, even in his last days, for speaking only the language of his people because very few could converse with him in Salish. I imagine there were times when endless days passed for him without the sound of another's voice, but the insistent language of his elders sustained him.

I arrived at his house in the mid-afternoon with Clarence Woodcock, the director of the Salish Culture Committee, as my interpreter. Blind Mose greeted us at the door with a gentle handshake of respect and welcomed us into his home. The light was so bright in the kitchen of the blind man that even after coming in from the midday sun, I squinted. I had expected his house to be dark, but I remember the radiant shine of his worn linoleum floors, here and there the blackened gleam of his tread. I have never been in a house so ordered and clean. In the bright stream of sun there were no dust motes. There was a light so clear, I believed he could see.

The pans that hung on the kitchen wall had been scrubbed thin and were shining like artist's silver. He had made coffee and it sat steaming on the stove in an oil-tin pot. The smell of cedar and tamarack smoke permeated the house and made me wistful. And his trademark, the black stovepipe hat trimmed by a lime green scarf, hung on the wall in the entryway. In old photos of the Flathead Reservation, Indians stand visiting in front of the St. Ignatius Mission, many wearing the same proud hat. And though I have never asked my elders, I believe Blind Mose was one of those men in the photographs even though that couldn't be possible because that would have made him almost 120 years old. He was never without that hat and only removed it when he entered the mission church. When Blind Mose died a few years after my visit, I was two thousand miles away in upstate New York and could not make it home for his wake and burial. But I knew that that hat was placed lovingly beside his hand for his last journey home.

Blind Mose did not have a living room. I don't remember seeing a couch or even a kitchen table. He invited us to sit in his bedroom. Two army blankets adorned two twin beds. He gestured for us to sit on the bed opposite him, and in that gesture I now recognize a generosity I have not encountered since. He was offering us all he had.

I cleared my throat and sat at the edge of the small bed, my back straight as a schoolgirl's. I looked for direction from Clarence on how I should comport myself, but Clarence sat with his back against the wall, his legs sprawled before him on the bed, comfortable and easy, smiling and sure. We sat for a long enough while that the loud summer day faded to silence. Clarence finally leaned forward, and the shifting of the bedsprings must have alerted Blind Mose because he cocked his head toward Clarence. Clarence introduced me as the great-great-granddaughter of Magpie Cap, the granddaughter of Annie Charlo, and I poised my pencil to my notebook ready for my elder's wisdom, but Blind Mose only nodded his head. Maybe he was not ready to speak, or maybe he was thinking about what he would say to us.

He crossed his legs at the ankle and hummed low. I shifted in the heat, noticed the yellowed blinds, the walls unadorned and peaceful. The day seemed suspended. I listened and was heartened to hear the mourning dove calling. I thought about this man living alone for years, hearing the burial songs over the graves of the Indians and whites who rested at the edge of his backyard. He must have heard, almost daily, the scrape of shovels just a step from his kitchen window. I wondered if spirits visited him, sought him out when the long nights settled.

That summer I worked for the Salish Culture Committee, cataloging grave sites that had been lost in allotment sales. I would spend long days in the old graveyards of Camas Prairie, stepping carefully between sinking graves and burial mounds to locate and mark the names of the people whose grave sites had been lost or forgotten.

After I had spent my first work week righting the bedpost head markers, mending the gray splintered crosses, and trying to read the faded names unprotected in their rain-riddled holders, I began to have my own visitors. I would be awakened every morning by two sound raps at my front door. My heart would lurch. I would tiptoe to the door, and pull back the curtain to reveal nothing. At the yard's edge, the moon-powdered light dimly lit the wild brush. The trunks of the large pines were still and ponderous.

When I heard the same rapping the next morning, I looked at the clock and noted the sound occurred at the same time as the previous visit. In the darkness I fumbled for the fire poker and went to the door. "Who's there?" I called. When there was no answer, I opened the door, brave with my newfound weapon, and was met by a chill breeze, a sound like low whispering, nothing but the star-haunted sky to greet.

I blamed my nephew for trying to scare me, not believing at first that I was being ghosted, even though my nephew swore he wasn't playing pranks on me. When Darren went away to basketball camp, the rapping persisted. Sometimes, I would hear knocking on the walls above my bed, and I would awaken startled and baffled. I wasn't sure what was happening to me. Clarence Woodcock said that the spirits followed me home from the graveyards because they wanted their stories to be told. "They didn't have a voice in this world," he said. "Now they have you."

A great horned owl perpetually perched on my fence post in the broad daylight and would circle me in flight whenever I stepped outside. I would peer out my back door, bewildered by the owl's constant vigil. Taps sounded at my windows, insistent. My family and friends visited and heard what I'd been hearing. But the night I saw blue-lit apparitions at my window, Clarence Woodcock came to bless my house. I had grown up with spirits and stories of spirits, and though I believed in the possibility of their existence and had even experienced their presence when I was younger, I had been too long away at school where no one spoke of such things. I had begun to turn away from the old ways and the teachings I had learned. I was afraid of the long nights alone, the spirits who followed me home. I was certain I was losing my mind. But that day, in the home of Blind Mose, in the summer of my haunting, I was comforted by the thought that he lived beside the dead. I imagined that he too felt the foot of his bed sag under the weight of a lonesome soul who had come to visit him.

Blind Mose finally spoke, and his voice was low and keening. He spoke in a way that still attends my dreams, a voice that was different in intonation from those of the native speakers of Salish today. If I were to describe his voice, I would say it sounded like prayer lifting; filmy, and yet solid, true to me as dirt. His speech would gutter in his throat and then recover, would be ghostlike and then return with vigor, a sound I can only liken to the beating of hawk's wings.

As he spoke I wanted to avert my eyes out of respect but could not. He was the eldest of our elders. Maybe for the first time in my life I recognized that I had to be a witness, that I could not let the image of his beautiful countenance fade before custom. I looked directly at him. His hair was white and unbound and hung almost to his waist with two warrior braids that framed his face. My mother said that Blind Mose had always been old, that when she was a young girl he looked the same to her as he did to me that day. His eyes were permanently closed, his lids as delicately luminous as pink shells. I put down my notebook and listened.

His father was a young boy traveling with a hunting party in the northern woods of what is now Idaho when they encountered the French fur trappers. They were camped on the shores of Lake Pend d'Oreille, and they were tired from hunting. They had been away from home for a long time. They were resting for a short while when they heard twigs snapping in the brush, the sound of strange voices coming toward them. They quickly hid in the trees and waited. The forest was dense with underbrush, so tight with trees the sunlight could not penetrate its depths. They couldn't see the men who were coming toward them. When they stepped from the shadow of the woods, Blind Mose's father gasped at the sight of them. The father had to cup his hand over his son's mouth to quiet him. Blind Mose said his father was startled by the color of the white men's skin, their loud voices in the clearing. The Indians believed the white men were wood spirits and they had disturbed them. Even though we'd been foretold of the white man's coming, the first sight was inconceivable.

I have heard other elders in our tribe say that Lewis and Clark were the first white men the Salish had ever seen, but I remember

Blind Mose's story. This summer marks twenty years since I sat in that small room and listened to Blind Mose tell the story that his father had told to him. Now I carry his father's story. If we mark history with our own memories and the memories others have passed to us, if all of our days can be measured by the length of a single person's life and the stories of the generation that precedes him, if twenty years passes with the same swiftness as a single day, then how quickly life turns. Two hundred years can be held in the living breath of one individual.

In the winter of 1804, Lewis and Clark were sheltered on the northeast bank of the Missouri at Fort Mandan, hunkered in for the first long winter of the expedition. The sky cracked with snow. Snow shattered in the twisting wind, and the Missouri River writhed black, then stilled. The men in the captains' charge suffered in the cold; their feet blistered from the ice-dry rub of their stiff-soled boots as they searched for game. The hunters, both Indian and white, returned to camp with little or no food and only a memory of the taste of bitter wolf meat.

Though Lewis and Clark were warm in their lodge and this was only the first winter of their travels, they must have believed their journey might end here or possibly never end. They must have known when the days dropped to twenty below zero, death was but a brief walk to the river or the wood bin. Frost jeweled the trees. Their lungs must have burned with each draw of breath. All day, all night, wood pitch hissed in the fireplace, chuffing ember-lit smoke to the snow-burdened sky. Clark's journal reveals the cruelty of the weather: "blew very hard last night, the frost fell like a Shower of Snow . . . Snow Drifting from one bottom to another." His journal became a catalog of the cold: "the Murcurey Stood this morning at 9 d below 0, December 29, 1804; Cold the Termtr. at 20 d below 0, December 30, 1804." On the last night of the year, Clark made particular note of the wind "mixed" with snow and sand, a stinging cold that must have seeped through the walls of their well-built dwellings. The misery of snow and sand relentlessly transformed even the river, so that it appeared to him as "hillocks of Sand on the ice, which is also Covered with Sand & Snow. . . ." As the sentence continues it betrays Clark's growing apprehension: "the frost which falls in the night continues on the earth & old Snow & c. & c."

When daylight closed, Clark must have absorbed himself with the calm of gathering information, playing board games, mapping the land to distract himself from the gloom of his days. But I imagine that in the queer snow-lit darkness, when all distractions failed him, Clark shifted his gaze to the firelit shadows and worried about all the things that could go wrong with the expedition.

In late November, an Indian man had stabbed and beaten his wife because one of the sergeants in the Corps had slept with her. When the woman ran away from her husband and showed up at the camp, Clark made promises then to the Indian man that his men would be punished if they slept with any married woman of the Indians. He promised the Mandan chiefs that he would protect them from their enemies. He ordered his own men to dance for the Indians in the hope that he could entertain them and divert their concerns from the troubles that threatened the camp. But the troubles continued. Clark's efforts proved futile. His men danced drunk with the wives of jealous Indians. Sentinels fell asleep on watch or neglected their duties altogether. Indian men continued to offer up women to the men in Clark's charge, hoping to capture the power they believed the white men held. Even the Indian man who had been jealous enough to beat and stab his wife for sleeping with one of the sergeants, returned to offer both of his wives.

That winter the river glazed over, dull gray and as spooky as a dead man's eyes. Smoke rose up off the backs of the shivering horses. At the ice-razored edge of a strange new land, the wind would suddenly hush. Because the land is never silent, Lewis and Clark had to have heard the frozen water scour and shriek like a woman as the currents roiled deep in the channel. They must have heard the long moan of water-logged cottonwoods in the evening when the temperature plunged. As the old year was passing, did they stir in sleep, split between half-waking and half-dreaming, hungry and homesick, and reflect upon the hardships that were yet to come?

They couldn't have been aware that north by northwest, over five hundred miles away, the Salish had begun their sacred winter dances. Lewis and Clark couldn't have known that a people they would meet in September of the new year were already praying for them. On December 30, 1804, in the Mandan camp, the thermometer dipped to twenty degrees below zero, but in less than forty-eight hours the temperature had dramatically risen by fifty-four degrees.

The dancer feels the slow draw of his blood in the cold day. The hunger that winter brings has made his knees weak, so he dances toward the hope of spring. A slow heat twitches in his heart and rises as he begins to pray.

On January 1, 1805, Clark observes, "The Day was worm [*sic*], Themtr. 34° abov 0," so warm the rain began to fall. Though the second and third day brought snow, Clark refers to the cold only once. On the fourth day of the new year, as the winter dance concludes, the temperature at Fort Mandan stood at twenty-eight degrees above zero. The cold returned again on the night of January 4, as the evening turned "cold and windey," but the prayers of the Bitterroot Salish had been answered. During the four-day duration of the winter dances, the Lewis and Clark party received a respite from the long cold spell.

Before the coming of the white man to the Bitterroot, Coyote blessed us with songs and medicine so that we might endure, rescued us from famine so that we would be wise hunters, sought to save us from death, and taught us that life endures. Coyote saved his people from the giants that threatened to consume us. In the Bitterroot and Jocko valleys, the mountains and rocks are physical testaments to the immensity of Coyote's battles. After he had slain the giants, he cast the great beasts into physical monuments that would attest to his victories. The monster rattlesnake's heart is still visible in the slope of the hills that border the town of Arlee, Montana. Sleeping Child remains at rest, a low butte swaddled in the soft yellow grasses above Hot Springs. Coyote slew the giants so that the Bitterroot Salish would know we can also conquer our greatest enemy. Through Coyote's example we recognize our greatest enemy is often ourselves. Because Coyote remains stingy, arrogant, and deceitful in the face of his triumphs, he suffers many deaths. But the people know if we bear all of Coyote's weaknesses, we must also possess his strengths. Every story reminds us that Coyote returned from the dead because he was given one friend who would always save him. When Coyote's tricks failed him and death would come, Fox would jump over Coyote's pitiful body and restore his life to him.

Every year when winter descends and frost laces the low valley trees, when the Flathead River slows with ice and ripples black, and the high mountains seem to carve the sky, the Salish people gather to pray. The Jump Dance begins the start of the year to renew and restore our lives. It is a dance of vision and prophecy. Through the dance we see what the new year will bring to the people.

We dance for good health and prosperity, not just for us but for all living things, all people. We dance to bring blessings to all the people whom we'll meet in the coming year. The prayer leader requests that we bring only good thoughts to the Jump Dance floor, that no tears be shed. If a dancer has difficulty, if his breath becomes labored or a sorrowful feeling comes to him in the dance, the prayer leader asks everyone to dance harder. "Pump your arms," he tells us. "Jump the people and yourselves through the bad times." If any dancer falters in the dance cycle, we know he will have difficulty in the new year. If he cannot continue the dance, we know the exact season of his death because it is marked by the cycle represented on the floor. We jump with vigor to recover our lives. We jump-dance over death and sorrow. We remember that Fox jumped over Coyote to bring him back to life.

Outside of the lodge, the day is warming. Snow is turning to slush from the heat of a thousand footsteps circling. Trees glitter with snowmelt as the prayers of the dancers lift. In the snapping lights of visions, in the chatter of whispered prayers, the dancer looks up to see the robe of light that surrounds him. The brilliant halo of the people's sweat is rising. Every hair on the dancer's head is singed with light. From under the cover of the lodge he spots the amber-gold flash of deer eyes. When the dancer's intentions are pure, he knows the animals will come to bless and feed the people. Lightning cracks the sky. The sound of thunder becomes the hooves of ten thousand buffalo striking hard ground.

The dancer has stepped into the cycle of summer. A hot wind seethes at his feet. Sweat glimmers at the small of his back. And a strange calm settles him. He can hear the breath puff of the dancers in front of him, the pump of dancers' arms behind him.

He sees the red fire of tamaracks, the blood of pitch. All the birds are still and quiet. Twigs snap beneath the hooves of deer. The buffalo are lifting their great heads toward something in the distance. He sees bears rise up on their haunches to sniff the air. He has never had a vision as powerful as the one before him. It is a vision of prophecy.

His hands tremble at his throat, but the vision does not leave him. He sees the trembling legs of deer, the twitching nostrils of elk. In the low hills the crows circle and call to the prairie dogs to hide. The rattlers are coiling, their tails buzzing the warning that he alone can hear.

Across the fields he sees them, the white men coming toward the people. He can see blood blue as the September sky in the map of their veins.

On a cold day in early September of 1805, Lewis and Clark did arrive in Flathead country. They were welcomed by the Salish and were offered white robes to rest upon and to take with them on their journey. Their visit was not remarkable, nothing monumental happened, but in many ways the exchange would prove significant. They left the Bitterroot friendship robes on the ground, perhaps the only things that the white people did not take from the original inhabitants of the Bitterroot Valley.

Chief Charlo and his people were eventually removed from their beloved homeland because the settlers Charlo would help and befriend wished to possess not only the land that they squatted on, but Charlo's land too. The white settlers acted on their greed. In 1872, just sixty-seven years after Lewis and Clark had arrived in the valley, everything the Bitterroot Salish held dear would be taken from

Chief Charlo with Secretary Garfield and their sons.
Courtesy K. Ross Toole Archives,
the University of Montana at Missoula.

them. James A. Garfield, the man who later became the twentieth president of the United States, fraudulently slashed Chief Charlo's *X* on the published document of the Hellgate Treaty, and the Bitterroot people were cheated out of their traditional homeland forever.

Like his father before him, Chief Charlo fought a fierce diplomatic battle to save his homelands for the future generations of his people. The white settlers were unharmed in his struggle. No blood was shed. In October of 1891, hungry and weary, his people starving and living in poverty, Charlo finally yielded and agreed to move his people to the Flathead Reservation. His exodus was a proud but solemn one. The Salish warriors dressed for war, but there was no war. The warriors guarded the people as they journeyed to their new homeland. When they reached Missoula, the warriors flanked the cross streets and halted traffic to spare the people the indignity of curious gawkers. They rode beside Charlo's procession, attempting to shield the people from the onlookers who lined the streets to witness their passing.

Chief Charlo leading the Salish from their Bitterroot home to the Flathead Reservation, October 1891. Mural by E. S. Paxson, courtesy of the Missoula Art Museum.

Chief Charlo was my great-great-grandfather. Paul Charlo, the last recognized chief of my people was my great-grandfather, the last in the traditional line of chiefs. As soon as Charlo passed the reservation boundary line, he stopped, refused to take even one more step away from the land that he loved. He never returned home again.

Charlo yearned for the Bitterroot Mountains and the valley of his people, but I have never felt sadness for the land my ancestors left behind. I have not longed to return to the Bitterroot Valley and have little desire to visit even now. I used to be troubled by the distance I felt, not in miles, but in spirit from the land my grandfathers fought to keep. I wondered why I felt no connection to my traditional homeland. I returned to the Bitterroot this winter, squinted into the sunlight that graced the mountains. I stood before the closed doors of St. Mary's Mission and tried to embrace the feelings Charlo had felt, but no grief tugged at me. Nothing. I felt numb in the face of the land my people had lost.

I visited my mother, and we talked about our lack of grief for the place we should long for. When someone passes from us, my mother said, the people protect the children so that they can move past their sorrow, so that they can forget the memories that would stir grief.

My mother was three years old when she suffered the death of her own mother. My grandmother, Annie Charlo, died young and beautiful at the age of twenty-nine when her lungs filled up with water thinner than tears. Pneumonia. My mother recollects only three memories of her mother. As her mother was dying, my mother perched on the steps that led to her mother's room. When my mother heard my great-grandmother cry, she stepped to the open door to see my great-grandmother holding her mother's hand. My mother remembers her own mother looking upward, her eyes luminous and hopeful. "Don't cry," she told my great-grandmother. "Look," she said. My mother glimpsed the ceiling but saw nothing. "I'm going to a beautiful place. The sky is so blue. Can you see it?" she whispered.

"There are colors I have never seen before." Annie Charlo died on a rain-drizzled day in early spring.

In my mother's second recollection it is summer. Her mother is in a dusty tent with her father. "I can still remember her laughter," my mother says. They had tied the tent flap shut, and they wouldn't let anyone in to disturb them. "I can still remember the sound of her laughter," my mother tells me. And my mother always smiles when she remembers her mother.

My mother carries one last memory of her mother. In this memory my mother stands beside the open grave of her own mother with her sisters and her grandmother. With ropes men are carefully lowering her mother's casket down into the grave. My mother hears thin streams of burial dirt slide downward like beads in talcum as her mother's casket comes to rest at the bottom of the grave. The prayer leader stands over the grave site and begins to pray. She smells the blessing of sweetgrass. Her mother is being sent on her final journey home. A man steps beside her grandmother and together they lift my mother up. "I fight them," my mother says, "when I begin to realize that they are going to pass me over my mother's open grave. I'm afraid they'll drop me. From across the open plot, the prayer leader is opening his arms to help me in the crossing. As I pass close by my mother for the last time, I look down to see her pine casket beneath me. Then the prayer leader has me tight in his arms, and I am safe."

The Bitterroot Salish pass a child over the grave of a parent so that the child will not be haunted by memories of the dead, which would prevent him or her from living happily and well. Very young children are passed over their mothers and fathers. My mother was passed over her mother's body, passed over sorrow, passed over sickness and trouble, passed over bad dreams and fears, passed over in the hope that she would not suffer the hardships of the past. Life passes over death so that the living can go on.

Charlo wanted his people to live in peace, to live without strife or the memory of his struggle. Before Charlo left his beloved homeland, I believe he asked the spiritual leaders and the medicine men to bless the people so that they could go on. As Charlo's people left the Bitterroot Valley, they passed over all the things that they loved. They passed over the graves of their grandmothers and grandfathers. The hallowed ground that they left behind was the dust of their ancestors. All they knew or would ever know came from the valley they were forced to leave.

When Charlo finally agreed to move from the Bitterroot, he carried the sorrow of his loss with him but did not pass his grief on. He must have prayed to the land to let his people live, to let his people kindly pass over the land that held them so that future generations could continue. Had we kept our desire knit to the land of our grandfathers and grandmothers, our yearnings would have destroyed us.

I have always been perturbed by the idea that Lewis and Clark had passed a great legacy on to all people. The University of Montana continues to employ the slogan "The Discovery Continues," refusing to see the irony of those words. Some years ago, I was asked to participate in a float trip down the Missouri River to experience the journey Lewis and Clark had made. At first, the idea seemed ridiculous: me drifting down the river, the lone Indian lifting my hand to point at the sights that Lewis and Clark had seen, an ignorant Sacajewea with no sense of direction. I wasn't going to go on the trip until Susan Stewart called me with plans to join the new discoverers. I had worked with Susan, a Crow Indian artist with a fierce heart, on the Montana Indian Contemporary Artists Council. I was still reluctant. If

I decided to go, at least I wouldn't be the only Indian. "Come on," she said. "It'll be fun."

Though I know very little about Lewis and Clark even now, I didn't know anything about Lewis and Clark then, not anything I could discuss with others anyway. I had vague images of two white men paddling a river, tromping through dusty woods, scared by and scaring the Indians they encountered. In my mind Sacajewea was a traitor, the woman who launched the parade of settlers who would come to claim our land. Lewis and Clark were a thousand road signs to me. *Here,* they said, *and over there too, we discovered you.*

The day before the trip, I read a few articles about the Corps of Discovery, bought an annotated version of the Lewis and Clark journals, and flipped through the pages, heckling the captains' spelling even though I am a disgraceful speller myself. I had never been on a float trip, never been on the Missouri River before that time or since. I worried about roughing it, squatting in the rattlesnake weeds to relieve myself. I didn't see the appeal in the journey at the time.

Days, we floated the shallow Missouri waters beneath a wood-blistering sun. Heat was a slow veiled breeze beneath the lip of the rubber raft gathering momentum without wind. Blue herons posed at the water's edge and turned their backs to us as we passed, thin and aloof as movie stars, unconcerned with our presence. I trailed my feet in the water as the raft drifted onward. Killdeer would streak the surface of the water, dip toward it as if bowing, suddenly lift without effort, wings folded tight, mirrored in the river as they darted past us. The river was the color of milky dark tea, in some places sleek and beaver brown, rippling in coves, slow-moving and powerful. Occasionally, I would jump from the rubber raft and let the current carry me along as I floated. I was able to move in front of the raft without effort, swimming like an Olympian in my mind. Susan would laugh at my dead man's float, kick water at me. "Woman overboard!" she would call to our river guides. "Woman down!"

When the other artists, as we were called, left the boat to hike the hot fields, we would decline. "Rattlers," we would say, lazy as lap dogs. We had no interest in "discovering" the land. We were Indians, after all. But the poet Sandra Alcosser would return with her journal full of specimens—silverweed and shepherd's purse, wild bergamot and sweet sage. I admired Sandra, and envied her. A brilliant poet. She would appear out of the desolate landscape, almost squealing in delight at her new finds, filled with ideas for whole books of poetry. I remained uninspired. We had been funded by the Montana Council for the Humanities and the Paris Gibson Square Museum to create something out of our experience on the river. I had nothing. Without wanting to, I tried to imagine what Lewis and Clark must have seen. The view from the river was the same view that they had seen—well, almost. The Missouri River of 1805 must have run clear, without the trailing dust of overgrazed fields, without the syrupy spittle of thirsty cattle. We didn't have to observe our surroundings through the lens of apprehension. We didn't have to worry about dwindling food sources or catching prairie dogs and pack rats to send back to the president.

The banks of the Missouri River from Fort Benton to Judith Landing have been almost destroyed by grazing herds of cattle. Cattle stood in the mud-sifted Missouri waters like lazy sentinels of progress. Every now and then a steer would spook as we passed by. Ten or more head would struggle to pull their hooves from the slurping sludge of eroded soil and charge away, leaving in their wake swirling dirty currents. I tried to envision a herd of buffalo on the plateaus, moving down to water; land without fences; river places absent of boat launches.

Our river guides were our Corps. With ceaseless grim smiles, they humped our belongings into and out of swollen rubber rafts, snapped white linen over card tables and made them glow with candlelight, prepared elaborate gourmet meals, woke us to steaming pots of coffee, custard toast, and friendly chatter. We gabbed endlessly beside the fires they had built, blathered about art and writing while the river men attended our coffee cups and wineglasses. When I borrowed one of the canoes and found I could not negotiate the current, the steadfast river guides stood on the riverbank and politely yelled instructions to me.

The last day of our journey, Susan and I began to talk about Lewis and Clark. We spoke mostly about Meriwether Lewis. I was struck by the irony of his name and the circumstances of his life and death. I was not fascinated with his life as much as I was interested in the mystery of his death, whether he was murdered or took his own life. I remembered his reflections on his thirty-first year: "I reflected that I had done very little, very little indeed, to further the happiness of the human race, or to advance information for succeeding generations," he wrote. I thought about Lewis, the long journey through the wilderness, the beauty and terror of his trip. He could not have passed over this land and not have wondered about what true effect he would have on the people whose lives he was disturbing. He must have realized, in quiet hours alone, that the path he had forged would later bring death and destruction to the Indians who had welcomed him into their villages. Then again, we reasoned, perhaps he didn't care. I wondered if he was cursed by the Indians, shot with thin medicine arrows that would conjure bad dreams, prophecies that would awaken in him when he returned home. His journey of discovery did "advance information" but not for the Indians. As the original captain of the Corps, he was the spearhead of Manifest Destiny.

On the last night of our own expedition, the sky turned ruddy, a slow wind picked up speed and the tents rippled, then flapped; a storm was coming. All my laziness over the past four days had made me tired. I crawled into the tent, ready for sleep. I awoke a few hours later. The suddenly stilled wind had left behind a suffocating heat. In the distance I could hear the rumbling earth. In short time, the tent flashed blue. And then the wind began to rush like cold, fast water. I scrambled out from under the aluminum frame, imagining the searing jump heat of ten thousand volts, the tent electrified, glowing red, my hair on fire.

"Get out!" I yelled to Susan. She turned in sleep and waved to me. A gunshot of lightning shattered the air close by, and she was up.

The other campers had gathered beside the river, everyone an expert on lightning storms. The sky cracked silver, and the rain fell hard. We were all gathered by the water, waiting to fry. The river guides headed for the lean-tos like GI Joes headed for cover. "Follow us!" they yelled back to the artists. People scarfed in sleeping bags ran after them.

I looked up the river. I have always been a person who enjoys the wonders of nature, the thrill of earth's devastating power. I have witnessed a wind shear buzz down one giant ponderosa after the other in my own backyard. I have seen a lightning strike explode into fire before me, but as I stood by the Missouri River that night my knees trembled at the sight coming toward me.

I have told this story many times; perhaps over the years I have embellished the tale, but I don't think so. As lightning blazed up the riverbanks, I saw flaring-fireball seconds on the water, silt-dust clouds exploding in dazzling brief light. I have heard that a man was once able to change the direction of wind by placing small flags on his walkway. I have seen the ghosts of the long-ago dead hovering at my windows. I have seen an owl swoop on a bat on a full-moon night, have heard the crunch of bat bones in his jaws. I have ducked beneath a thin blanket in the back of my Dad's El Camino while an owl has passed over me, his wingspan covering every inch of me and the pickup bed. I have heard the gargled voice of a man near death. I have seen my dead husband walking on the streets of New York, but I have never witnessed anything like what I saw that night.

It was not lightning. I saw a giant man electrified. Each spear of lightning was he, illuminated. Every electrified hit was he, stepping closer. He lit the river and the pale cliffs like daylight. As I made my way to the lean-to, I turned to see him pass by the camp and move onward down the Missouri.

If the old stories are true and prophecy exists for the people, nature shows us what the future holds.

WHO'S YOUR DADDY?

Mark N. Trahant

MARK N. TRAHANT is a member of Idaho's Shoshone-Bannock Tribe. He is also editor of the editorial page for the *Seattle Post-Intelligencer.* In this capacity he chairs the daily meeting of the editorial board, directing a staff of writers, editors, and a cartoonist, and contributes a weekly Sunday column on issues ranging from family to democracy.

Trahant is one of the nation's most experienced Indian working journalists and newspaper executives. He has been a reporter for the *Arizona Republic* in Phoenix, executive news editor at the *Salt Lake Tribune,* publisher of the *Moscow-Pullman Daily News* in Moscow, Idaho, as well as editor and publisher of several tribal newspapers, and, most prominently, he is a former president of the Native American Journalists Association. Trahant also has a scholar's interest in his tradition and professional past, as evidenced in his *Pictures of Our Nobler Selves,* a history of American Indian contributions to journalism, published in consequence of his appointment as a visiting scholar at the Freedom Forum First Amendment Center at Vanderbilt University.

Mark N. Trahant's Lewis and Clark connections are significant, though not currently geographical, since he lives with his family well north of the Columbia River, on Bainbridge Island in Washington.

WHO'S YOUR DADDY?

Lewis and Clark, Told as a Family Story

When I was a little boy, my grandmother told me we were related to Lewis and Clark. The story started after we passed a road sign in southern Idaho, one marking the Lewis and Clark trail. Or, it might have been after someone read a newspaper article. But whatever the reference, after it was made, my grandmother would add, quite casually, that we were supposed to be related to Lewis and Clark. "Our name is Clark," she'd say. "We are all Clarks."

My first memory of this conversation begins at age six, seven, or something like that. I am not all that certain—my memory is hazy— but I recollect a hot, sunny day on my grandmother's porch in Fort Hall, Idaho, and overhearing a story about some "Lewis Ann" fellow. I wondered why he had "Ann" as a middle name.

I was immediately corrected the first time I mentioned my concern (accompanied by a chorus of laughter). There was no Lewis Ann. Only those two explorers named Lewis and Clark. I then understood that it was William Clark who might be our relative, or, as my grandmother put it, "We are all Clarks."

Could it be? Is Captain William Clark my pa? (Technically: my daddy's great-great-great-grandfather.) But this very idea adds a twist to the concept that we are all related; it makes the possibility literal.

I thought of my grandmother's supposed relative a few years ago when I took my family to a Lewis and Clark site. It was one of those glorious Idaho summer days. We drove up the dirt road to Lemhi Pass, where I tried to talk to my two boys about this place and what it might mean. (I will know only a decade or two from now if they heard anything, or if they did, what they will remember.)

At the end of the trail, we walked around, then stood on a ridge, surrounded by fields of yellow, purple, and white wildflowers. It was as if history had an echo: far off from our warm skies, thunderstorms marched in our direction; the sound of that advance rumbled back and forth across nearby canyon walls.

"After refreshing ourselves we proceeded to the top of the dividing ridge from which I discovered immence [*sic*] ranges of high mountains still to the West of us partially covered with snow," wrote Captain Meriwether Lewis in his journal. "I now descended the mountain about ¾s of a mile which I found much steeper than on the opposite side, to a handsome bold running creek of cold clear water. Here I first tasted the water of the great Columbia River."

I walked over to a creek, a trickle, really. I know that the water from this creek flows into the Lemhi River on its long journey to the Columbia and then to the Pacific.

This ridge, this water, and my family stand at this very point of intersection with history. The story is personal, not merely some abstraction. Most of the history we know comes from the pages of a book, often assigned to us long ago during a classroom exercise. The result is a dry narrative, a basic list of names and places with little relevance to our life in the present. But what if the story has a familiarity? Does history change if we think not only of the primary characters, but what our family might have been doing, too? Where were those who we think of as "ours"?

At the very least, for my family, this intersection is interesting because the travelers that crossed here altered the landscape.

"This is where the world changed," I told my two sons, as we surveyed Lemhi Pass. The traffic that passed here is as busy and crowded as our ancestry. My father's family is Assiniboine, Shoshone-Bannock, French, and English. My mother's heritage is Scottish and English. My children add Navajo to that exchange. Somewhere in that gridlock, I was told as a child, are the Clarks.

So many different travelers: warriors, explorers, trappers, pioneers, and settlers, all a part of a family's journey in the American West. Each traveler tells a story along the route, stories that are sometimes in competition with one another. They say, "Winners write history." And I suppose that's true because it's the winners' versions that outline the drafts that follow. These are the master narratives, told as part of a nation's mythology.

But eventually other stories surface, too. These alternative histories serve as reminders that the journey continues, that there's a generational legacy that's passed along in several directions. My story is one that comes from my family. It's a narrative of travel, a story of the ancestors who survived. That might not seem remarkable today because we are all related to the survivors. But consider the odds of that survival two centuries ago.

My ancestors lived through terrible encounters with smallpox. A major epidemic swept through Shoshone country (as well as through the lands of their allies and enemies) around 1780. In her book, *Pox Americana*, Elizabeth Fenn describes how quickly the disease spread across a Shoshone trade route that stretched in four directions, from the southern plains, on into Mexico, throughout the Northwest Plateau, and into Canada. She writes that there is no mortality data for the Shoshone, but she believes all the tribes from the southern and northern plains and the Northwest Plateau incurred more than fifty thousand deaths.

From the Assiniboine side of my family, the stories have more specificity. Tribal historian Robert Fourstar wrote: "Smallpox epidemics came to our people three times. The first time approximately half of our people perished. Entire bands died." He said warriors would prove their fearlessness by wearing the robes of victims—resulting in even more deaths from the disease.

The sheer enormity of the societal earthquake is beyond imagination. Just think about those three words: "Entire bands died." "Entire bands died" meant ceremonies died, too, because rituals were often entrusted to a particular group. "Entire bands died" would have meant poverty for the survivors. "Entire bands died" meant that territory that had been protected for generations was lost in one instant to enemies.

The smallpox epidemic devastated most tribes, while, conversely, a few tribes benefited (at least in the short term). It all depended on who was where when the virus was propagating.

I have to think, despite the lack of mortality data, that the Shoshone world must have still been reeling when it encountered the Corps of Discovery. This might explain why Lewis described the band he met—the Agaidika—as poor and hungry. This band, the "salmon-eaters," or now sometimes known as Lemhi Shoshone, might have been a group directly unaffected by the so recent epidemic—yet even they must have been still dealing with the consequences. Some speculate that an entire band of Shoshone (one similar to the mountain Agaidika band), which inhabited what is now Yellowstone National Park, was completely destroyed by smallpox. The Agaidika might have escaped direct contamination, because if they had had visible marks, that is certainly something that Lewis would have observed and recorded. But the indirect consequences of the smallpox must have impacted every Shoshone band—as well as every trading partner.

As I showed my children Lemhi Pass, I had to think of this place as one for those who endure. We are all descended from smallpox survivors; we are the ones who lived. Somehow our ancestors defeated the most deadly of enemies. Yet I don't have a literal tie to what happened at Lemhi Pass (unless my grandmother is right about Clark) because my ancestors weren't there. My ancestors were not Shoshone; they were Bannock. And they were more likely traveling somewhere in the Great Basin (although even then there was a great deal of back-and-forth between different bands and allies).

But this story goes beyond just what happened on the day of that encounter between the Corps and the Shoshone because my family's version of the story contains an alternative chapter that should be included in the narrative drafted by Lewis and Clark. In the journals, Lewis's observation about Shoshone poverty comes to be accepted as truth. He wrote down what he saw that day, his point of view limited in scope. But he also trips across another version, not recognizing what he might have seen had he had a wider lens.

While hunger and poverty defined Shoshone life, at least in Lewis's eyes, he somehow misses the significance of, and then dismisses, similarly apparent signs of wealth. "The tippet of the Snake Indians is the most elegant piece of Indian dress I ever saw," Lewis wrote in his journal on August 20. "The neck or collar of this is formed of a strip of dressed otter skin with the fur . . . and has the appearance of a short cloak and is really handsome."

The four hundred "fine" horses owned by the Agaidika band impressed several men in the Corps. Lewis recognized Spanish brands on the animals. "I also saw a bridle bit of Spanish manufactory, and sundry other articles which I have no doubt were obtained from the same source," he writes in the journal. But then, in the very next sentence, Lewis reaches the polar conclusion of the Agaidika's extreme poverty.

Did he ever wonder about this contradiction? Lewis described articles that could have been part of a Shoshone trading system—and the fine horses could have been the indication. The trading system, too, fits with the setback from the smallpox because contact with other tribes and trading partners helped spread the disease so quickly throughout the region.

Sometime later Lewis and Clark should have figured out their mistaken impression on their own. When the Corps bargained for horses, they simply were matched against better traders. The twenty-nine horses Lewis and Clark bought "nearly all had sore backs," according to historian James Ronda. In the Shoshone world, it was a good story to be told: how they sold the captains the band's worst horses.

There's another contradiction in the Lewis and Clark narrative that directly challenges the stories I understand to be true. In Stephen Ambrose's *Undaunted Courage,* we are told of two "firsts" that began with the 1804 death of Sergeant Charles Floyd. "On August 20, Floyd died, most likely from peritonitis resulting from an infected appendix that had perforated or ruptured. Sergeant Floyd was the first U.S. soldier to die west of the Mississippi," Ambrose wrote. "Two days and forty-one miles later, the captains ordered an election for Floyd's replacement. Private Patrick Gass got nineteen votes, while Privates William Bratton and George Gibson split the remainder. This was the first election ever held west of the Mississippi."

These two firsts pose an epistemological challenge: How do we know what we know? How do we measure what's known about the Corps of Discovery journey versus everything that unfolded during the same era with far less fanfare? Someone else could easily have been the first—what if some soldier boy just wandered off and died?

The second issue troubles me far more because it raises questions about the very legitimacy of democracy. A historical marker along U.S. 20 near the Nebraska Bluffs marks August 22, 1804, as the place and date of "the first election held west of the Mississippi." This is the narrative of the colonialist. The Corps did something noble, unique, enlightened, progressive, and of course, democratic. But what if democracy was already present, just in a different form?

Democracy scholar Robert Maynard Hutchins once defined it this way: "Every member of the community must have a part in his government. The real test of democracy is the extent to which everybody in society is involved in effective political discussion." By that definition many, if not most, or even all, American Indian nations, tribes, and bands were democratic from the beginning of time.

The Shoshone band that met the Corps of Discovery already had a democratic system in place. The methods of leadership suited the people and the band's collective ambition. Again, Lewis gives us a hint in his journal that he saw a glimmer of this notion. After again mentioning the Shoshones' "extreme poverty," Lewis writes, "Each individual is his own sovereign master and acts from the dictates of his own mind; the authority, of the cheif [*sic*] being nothin' more than mere admonition supported by the influence which the propriety of his own exemplary conduct may have acquired him in the minds of the individuals who compose the band."

Lewis goes on to say that the chief is not a hereditary post, but one earned through influence. Indeed, as I understand it, every man was a chief in some respects. Shoshone leadership was about following leaders focused on specific tasks. Much has been written about the notion of peace chiefs or war chiefs, but the concept was much more comprehensive. A band's leader that day or week might be a "fish boss," who would guide a group to fish when the salmon runs were abundant. Then someone else would step in as a leader for a different task.

The people were always choosing the leader they wanted to follow—and if not, they'd simply move on to another leader or even another band. Again, if you take fishing as an example, some leaders were quite good at constructing weirs, or small dams, that blocked fish during their migratory run. Others preferred to hunt the salmon, chasing them up a river with spear poles. The governance of these bands was, by any definition, democratic. "Elections" were held often—essentially when a specific task was needed. People voted by their participation.

The very foundation of the Shoshone democratic tradition was not the representative model used by the Americans. It was based on a different way of thinking. But the differences between the two approaches were ignored in the first draft of the American master narrative. Instead the story becomes flatter, a simpler form; it becomes the overreaching "our way is democratic, yours is not."

This narrative preceded Lewis and Clark, of course. Thomas Jefferson, the Corps' sponsor, was keen on the promise of "civilization." Yet he ignored the Constitution and his own religious (or nonreligious) beliefs when he drafted and sent Christian missionaries to carry out this scheme. The First Amendment prohibited "establishment" of a state religion, which would have been news in Indian country because missionaries were often the willing tools of the civilization policy. Even in that era, various thinkers didn't like the idea. Writer and social critic Thomas Paine warned the government to "keep a strict eye over those missionary societies, who, under the pretense of instructing the Indians, send spies into their country to find out the best lands." The canyon that divides my family story and the American "official" version originates here. The Lewis and Clark narrative made evident that its writers did not comprehend either the indigenous belief system or the democracy that was already present. The journals suggest the authors' own intellectual poverty because their interpretation missed the gems of a fine and handsome system already in place.

This initial distortion worsens with every telling. Every layer of the story covers the original truth even more. In later versions, the Americans would argue for democracy, while really seeking a dictator. They wanted a top boss, someone who could speak (and sign treaties) for every band of Shoshones. The government never found that warped version of the story, that kind of boss with every power delegated to him by his people.

This confusing narrative explains why there's continued tension about tribal leadership even today: the same American government that could not comprehend a native democracy went about promoting their own brand of "self-determination" or local democracy to Indian people across the country, setting up a conflict with the homegrown variety.

Another layer of this same story was told in 1934 when Congress enacted the Wheeler-Howard, or Indian Reorganization, Act. This time the call for a "first" democracy was part of President Roosevelt's Indian reforms, led by John Collier at the Bureau of Indian Affairs.

My grandfather's cousin was a man by the name of George P. Lavatta. (To confuse things a little: our common ancestor had two different wives; George's grandmother was Shoshone, while my great-great-grandmother was Bannock, but no matter the relationship, I called him Uncle.) Lavatta had gone to the Carlisle Indian School and had built a successful career at Union Pacific, starting as a day laborer and working his way into management as the "advisor general" on Indian matters for Union Pacific's president Carl Gray. When I asked Uncle what he did, he'd always reply that he was "organizing." When folks needed housing, they'd get a committee together. Or when more jobs were needed, they'd get a committee together.

He said that when Shoshone-Bannocks first started working at the railroad they organized—and sent candy to the employees' children. This was the Depression era, and jobs were scarce. "So when the

Indians came in to work, hell, they welcomed them with open arms. No one resented it at all. They weren't taking nobody's jobs."

Lavatta left the railroad for the Indian Service in 1929. His job, once again, was organizing Indians, recruiting them into the workforce. "There is just one way of solving the Indian problem. It isn't to sympathize with the 'poor, downtrodden Indian' and make him think that the world owes him a living," Lavatta said. "The answer is: 'Give them a chance to work—and make them work.' " Collier's notion of democracy—and my uncle's ideas about work, organizing, and the future of Indian country—fit exactly with that era.

"John Collier, I admire that man so much," my uncle told me. "He wanted me to have more to say. And, boy, that's the reason he warms the cockles of my heart." Lavatta recalled a plan he had for organizing, one that he told Collier about. "We were talking to him about it. He was for it. He said wonderful, go right ahead." By 1935 George P. Lavatta was a government salesman for democracy. It was his mission to convince tribes to accept the Indian Reorganization Act and to pass a constitution. My uncle was based in Portland, but he traveled to reservations throughout the Northwest, explaining a "better" form of government. The Shoshone-Bannock Tribes adopted an IRA constitution—but that document did not bring about the sort of participation that Lavatta and others expected.

In August of 1937, on a Pocatello, Idaho, radio show, Lavatta said it was still "unusual" for tribal members to be asked their wishes by their government. "Due to their lack of understanding as well as lack of opportunities to participate in the past, a great deal of interest was not shown by the Indians in the various districts in the first election, which was held for representative council members." Lavatta complained that at tribal meetings the Indian Affairs superintendent did too much of the talking. But, he said, "when the time came for the Indians to consider and discuss among themselves the contents as well as the benefits of the Reorganization Act, they were ready and at once realized the great opportunity that was being provided, and they readily accepted."

The Indian Reorganization Act allowed tribes to say yes or no. And many tribes enacted variations from the model constitution, while others passed and came up with other forms of governance. The constitutional model that some tribes—including the Shoshone-Bannock Tribes—appropriated the idea of "checks and balances" from the U.S. Constitution, with a colonial twist. The official governing council would be an elected body, but before laws, ordinances, or contracts could be put into effect, the council was required to send the paperwork for approval to the U.S. secretary of the interior (or a designate). In effect: the U.S. government decided it should serve as the check and the balance.

Lavatta was for the organization of an intertribal democracy, too. In 1944 he was one of the founders of the National Congress of American Indians. But, if anything, my uncle was a paradox. I think he instinctively understood the democratic process—and must have known, deep down, that Indians had always been democratic. His actions trumped his boarding-school education: He was always organizing; forming a committee, ready to act. He would have found a way to get people together to solve problems, no matter what form government took.

I remember one time seeing him, long after he retired, at a meeting of Idaho tribes. At a quarter to eight, shortly before the meeting was to begin, Uncle George wandered the halls, shouting loudly: "C'mon, everybody. It's time to start. Time to get moving." I caught the sense of urgency in his voice. That meeting (perhaps any meeting) was important. The People (the noun used in its most elegant form) had business before them. This was democracy in action.

Yet he was a strident voice of the BIA party line, buying into the mythology that democracy was the American gift. A story my uncle told me hints at this absurdity. He worked for the Bureau of Indian Affairs during the time when the U.S. government was terminating its relationship with tribes. As with the IRA, tribes could vote to terminate or continue the relationship with the government. The policy was designed to get the federal government out of Indian business or, some said, to "free the Indians."

I asked my uncle what that was like. He said he tried to think about how Indians would gain—or suffer. "We've got some wonderful people in the Indian bureau, got some wonderful boys," he said. "Then we've got some damn stinkers." He then spoke of meeting with the Klamath Tribe as they considered their termination vote. "I talked to them with tears in my eyes, trying to get them to not terminate. I said, 'You're not ready.' " That was the party line. He said, "You're not ready," instead of "It's none of your business." The American government had the answers.

On that Oregon reservation, the tribal members with direct ties to Washington supporters of termination carried the day. The democratic United States forced a disastrous policy on the Klamath (and then on other tribes). The "damn stinkers" won.

What I find interesting, looking back on the Indian Reorganization Act, comes to the question of democracy—and its definition. My uncle could accept the "You're not ready," but he didn't see what was there before John Collier, the Indian Reorganization Act, and even the civilization that so impressed him at Carlisle School. Some seven decades after the IRA, there is nothing that shows the tribes with the model constitutions to be any more democratic. Indeed, I think many of the tribes that rejected the formatted constitutions have been among the more innovative and representative, including the United States' largest tribe, the Navajo Nation.

Democracy, termination, and the mythological first election are legacies of my family—and the telling of the Lewis and Clark story. That takes me back to the mountain, to Lemhi Pass. I wonder again about my grandmother's story. Was my family here? For a long time I have doubted the story. It didn't seem right. How could William Clark have been our relation?

Recently I decided to treat this family story as a mystery, to look for the facts and try to set the story right. William Clark, of course, spent time in the Milk River country, starting with the Corps of Discovery. But he was far too old to have been Walter Clark's father. My great-grandfather was born in 1871, and William Clark died in 1838.

My first question, then, is could Clark have been a father to some future heir around the time the Corps of Discovery visited the Assiniboine? This is impossible as well because of the mathematics involved. The government census lists Walter Clark as one-half Assiniboine. It's clear he had a white father and an Indian mother—the only alternative would have been a lineage involving (precisely) a half-degree father, half-degree mother, half-degree grandfather, and half-degree grandmother. That straight one-half combination seems remote in the world of love—especially over two generations. Another problem with that idea is that as late as 1881, Walter Clark did not even have an English name. So that entire line of thinking seems unlikely.

Another family story says Walter's father was a "Major Charles Clark." A quick look at Montana history shows all sorts of Charles Clarks—one a mining heir, another a Buffalo soldier, and a third a rascal. But none of the dates—at least of the known characters—quite match up.

There's also a problem with geography. The Fort Peck Indian (Assiniboine and Sioux Tribes) Reservation in the Milk River area, even today, is remote. It's a long drive from Billings—or anywhere else. I can only imagine how far off it must have seemed back then. In 1869 a government report from the Montana superintendent omits any information about Fort Peck because, he writes, "I have no report from their agent in regard to the Indians." Then the superintendent adds, "Many Indians live on the British side of the line." I look through the Assiniboine census of 1875 and see no clues at all. There's no Walter Clark—the males about his age were often called "The Boy" or "Good Boy," and several were pegged as "Bad Boy."

I find references to Walter Clark beginning in 1881. He's listed in a group of four: his mother, Kanigiwinceisea, or "the Gone Girl" in English; Walter Clark, age thirteen; Thomas Campbell, age seven; and Sarah Campbell, age twelve. The survey is the same the following

Walter Clark, 1917.
Trahant family photograph.

year, except my grandmother's name is changed to Naya Calhaza or "Left Girl," or possibly "Left Behind Girl."

The next census lists her name as "Mrs. Flynn" both on the Indian line and on the English line. Her two younger children's names were changed to reflect this change in marital status; they became Thomas Flynn and Sarah Flynn. (My grandmother remembered her only as Grandma Flynn.) Walter Clark remains Walter Clark. He was the only member of the family to stick with his identity. He was seventeen.

None of the records, the agent's reports, or any other scrap of paper reflects any linkage with William Clark. There's only that family story—and a bit of "red hair." My grandmother's sister was a red-headed Indian—and the red-hair genes were something that my grandmother claimed as part of her lineage.

The red hair is where the William Clark story becomes remote, but possible.

William Clark had a grandson by the name of Charles Jefferson Clark, the son of Meriwether Lewis Clark. Charles would have been about the right age: in fact, he married a woman in Kentucky, Lena Jacob, in 1873, which was about two years after Walter Clark was born.

But I don't know if Charles Clark was ever in Montana—and the geography is a formidable barrier. I also have found no evidence that Charles would have been a major (although his father was a brigadier general for the Missouri militia and a Confederate colonel. He lost his older brother fighting for the South at the battle of Pea Ridge in Arkansas. So a military commission is something that could have occurred).

But without more evidence, Charles Clark's life seems awfully removed from that of a Montana Indian reservation. I just don't see the fit.

I also wonder about another part of my family's stories: My great-grandfather would have been alive during 1904 and 1905—a time when there was a great deal of talk about Lewis and Clark.

My grandmother once gave me an old photograph. It was a faded, black-and-white copy (or more likely, a copy of a copy) of a horse-drawn buggy surrounded by sagebrush. Inside the carriage sat two stylish women and a young child. A train was in the background with

Genie Butch, Josephine Butch Clark, and Walter Clark, Jr., as a baby.
The man is unidentified. The picture was taken around 1910.
Trahant family photograph.

one of the cars labeled "Photographing and Dental Co." On the back of the photograph, in my grandmother's handwriting, it reads: "Mother, Walter, Jr. and Aunt Genie."

I knew my Aunt Genie only through newspaper clips. From time to time, the newspaper from my grandmother's tribe, *Wotanin Wowapi*, would publish old photos. Once there was a picture of Aunt Genie in a buckskin dress along with seven other young women. Another time there was a picture of her and some other women in what looked like sailor suits, but they were wearing the basketball uniforms of that age. The caption credited the Fort Peck Tribal Archives and told little else, other than that this picture was a girls' basketball team from a government boarding school around the turn of the century. I remember peppering my grandmother with all the wrong questions. I wanted to know about the train, the photographing and dental company, and where they might be headed. I wanted to know what it was like back then.

But I should have been asking about Aunt Genie. This picture might have been taken when Genie was on her way to take a train, perhaps to play a basketball game. Like so many young men and women of that era, Genie Butch was sent to a government school at Fort Shaw, Montana (about twenty-five miles north of Great Falls). One of the main schools at Fort Peck had burned down in 1892, so pretty much all school-age children were sent away to these "industrial schools" where the course work was designed to "civilize" young Indians. In 1902 the school started a girls' basketball team. They were good enough to play colleges and other Montana teams. A couple of years later, it was clear the team was better than anyone imagined because they won every game they played. The team's legend was such that it was invited to compete at the 1904 World's Fair, the Louisiana Purchase Exposition in St. Louis, Missouri. A group of girls ranging in age from twelve to eighteen traveled by train from Montana, stopping at towns along the way to play challengers. At the World's Fair, the team won every game and was crowned 1904 Champions of the World (basketball was not then an Olympic sport—or the team probably would have won gold medals, too).

The team was popular with fans. The games were played outdoors, and the court had to be roped off just to keep the crowds at a decent distance. One St. Louis enthusiast is reported to have said he stayed an extra day at the fair just to see Fort Shaw play. He praised the Fort Shaw team as easily the best in the world. A year later the team traveled to Portland to challenge teams at the 1905 Lewis and Clark Exposition. "They found no teams willing to accept their challenge, but a side trip to Salem, Ore., pitted them against the only Indian girls team they ever met, the Chemewa Indian School," says a story in the Montana Historical Society newsletter. "Fort Shaw triumphed again."

For me, the triumph is the family stories. This is also the best evidence, I think, that we're not related to Captain Clark. My grandmother's aunt must have told great stories about going to the world's fairs in St. Louis and Portland. If we were related to Clark (although it would have been Genie's brother-in-law who was related), it seems to me that it would have been part of the conversation. How could my aunt have traveled to Portland's exposition and not brought home trinkets? There should have been "stuff" that would have been incorporated into the family stories. (Then, again, perhaps Walter Clark was uncomfortable talking about any connection to his father. My grandmother rarely talked about who her grandfather might be. She just didn't know.)

Something else was going on in our family about the same time as the St. Louis World's Fair. My great-grandfather hosted his own celebration. Walter Clark married Josephine Butch. They had eleven children and were doing quite well on the Fort Peck Indian Reservation (then only about twenty-five years old).

Still, life was tough, the family had lost two children, and a third, Walter, Jr., was gravely ill. My great-grandfather, who was also known as Chabaza or Stockade, made a vow to the Creator. Make his son well, he prayed, and he would celebrate his son's life with a ceremony. He promised a big celebration—a feast, dance, and giveaway—for all those who could come.

His and my great-grandmother's prayers were answered. The young boy was restored to health. So they invited people to his celebration, and folks came from all over the region and Canada. My great-grandparents fed everyone, butchering cows as people arrived. They provided shelter, tents or tepees for those who did not bring their own. And they gave away amazing things: blankets, clothes, and horses.

When my grandmother used to tell me this story, she would pause after talking about giving away horses. In those days, she used to say, giving away a horse was like giving away a truck or a car today. Sometimes gifts were given to people who had worked hard at helping others. Or they could have been given to those who really needed them for one reason or another. Or the gifts could go to people who my great-grandparents did not even know.

Nowadays when people talk about Walter Clark, they talk of him as a wealthy man. But the judging of his wealth wasn't in the terms of being a millionaire or of what he had; he was wealthy because he gave so much away. Sometimes, my grandmother told me, her father traveled to town in his wagon to buy groceries—only to give them all away before he returned home, his wagon still empty. She told me people would visit her house and bring their problems, day or night. Her parents would feed them, listen, and try to help. (My grandmother said this was the reason that she couldn't wait to go away to boarding school; she was tired of always cooking for people.)

These are the family stories that tell of character. But they also pose a challenge, incorporated through narrative, passed along to every descendant. Now, when we give away something, we honor our great-grandparents. My family honored our ancestors a few years ago. The Red Bottom Powwow—named for the Red Bottom Clan of Assniboine—had its one hundredth anniversary. The powwow has continued every year (except during World War II), always organized by Clark family members and others in the community. Some do it because it's a community tradition, but others contribute because they are fulfilling their ancestor's vow.

This family's legacy and our stories continue. At Red Bottom, we joined many other descendants of Walter Clark and Josephine Butch. At the celebration, we gathered. We prayed. We danced. We ate, and we fed people. We swapped stories with family members with whom we are close and with relatives we were meeting for the first time. We also gave away a stack of gifts, handed out to those who joined the celebration. It was such fun to shop for things that would be gifts; somehow it means even more when you never know who received them. We didn't give away any cars, but I think my great-grandfather would have been proud of the gifts.

So much of the celebration, at least for me, was the memory of my grandmother and her telling of our stories. It was a way to put places or events into a context of meaning. It doesn't matter when the first celebration occurred; it matters that the celebration continues. This was a new telling of an old story. We were part of a large family—grandparents, fathers, mothers, uncles, aunts, siblings, and cousins—keeping alive a prayer and a vow. This is how this story is passed along to the next generation, a ceremony for my children as they navigate life.

It is because of this celebration, and our family stories, that we will always know we are all Clarks.

MERIWETHER AND BILLY
AND THE INDIAN BUSINESS

Bill Yellowtail

BILL YELLOWTAIL, Crow, grew up on his family's cattle ranch on the Crow Indian Reservation in Montana. Although the letters A.B. denote his degree attainment at Dartmouth College (1971), an acronymic EPEF (Education, Politics, Environment, Fishing) in many ways sums up his lifelong pursuits since then. Yellowtail's first major responsibility in education was as assistant supervisor of Indian education in the Montana Department of Public Instruction, where he not only administered a $1 million grant program but also wrote the curriculum in Indian Studies for public-school teachers.

From there he moved back to the Crow Agency, where he again administered a variety of educational projects as director of Human Resources Development and Education. More and more prominent in Montana public life, Bill Yellowtail went all the way into politics with his election in 1984 (re-elected in 1988 and 1992) to the Montana State Senate, representing Big Horn, Rosebud, and Powder River counties. He served on a number of committees, two especially involving his interest in the environment. No doubt this activity as well as a strong personal background led to his appointment, in 1994, by then EPA administrator Carol Browner, as regional administrator responsible for a six-state region, including Montana, Wyoming, Utah, Colorado, and the Dakotas.

If the Crow Indians in Lewis and Clark's day were renowned for their knowledge of horses and horsemanship, Yellowtail is a most remarkable and dedicated fly fisherman and winner of the 1991 Angler of the Year Award from *Fly Rod and Reel* magazine. He lives in Bozeman, Montana, with his spouse, Margarette Carlson, who is a painter, sculptor, and fine-arts teacher.

MERIWETHER AND BILLY
AND THE INDIAN BUSINESS

O n July 25, 1806, Captain William Clark participated generously in the economy of the Yellowstone River region. That his contribution was nocturnal and not entirely voluntary is not material to this story. Delivery of fifty head of prized Nez Perce horses to the local trade network was what counted.

Clark never actually met his counterparts in the transaction. Perhaps he was a trifle hasty in his assumption that the entrepreneurs with whom he dealt were Crow Indians. But to give him his due, he was merely extrapolating from the widely celebrated Crow penchant for fine horses and their enterprising nature in pursuit thereof.

No legends of the encounter survive in the tribal archive to corroborate Clark's attribution. But the Crows are prone to modesty, and besides, it was business as usual. Clark was exploring the Yellowstone during his return to "civilization," having divided the Corps of Discovery with Meriwether Lewis. Lewis, for his part, contributed a few horses to the Blackfeet economy on his loop north of the Missouri. Both parties stoically bade their investments adieu and proceeded onward in their accustomed dugout canoes and bull boats.

INDIAN BUSINESS

The vital common thread for the captains' reportage to President Thomas Jefferson was that Native inhabitants throughout Louisiana Territory were a thoroughly independent, businesslike lot—sharp entrepreneurs and shrewd dealers. Lewis and Clark got along best when they respected and participated in the established trade economies, as they did while wintering over among the Mandans and Hidatsas. There they fabricated iron implements at their own portable forge to barter for the staple commodities of corn and squash that sustained them through the bitterly cold winter of 1804–1805. Lewis was astonished to arrive in the Nez Perce community a few months and a thousand miles later only to find that one of these trade axes had actually preceded him! The journals leave it to us to speculate upon the chain of transactions that brought it there.

By contrast, the Corps' early and nearly fatal encounter with the Teton Sioux was a result of Lewis's brash announcement that the United States would now be taking charge of commerce in the region. Incensed, the Tetons proposed to eradicate this arrogant intrusion upon the extensive and finely tuned regional trade network that the Sioux had worked hard to facilitate. By that harsh lesson Lewis learned to approach the local trade czars with considerably more deference and economic diplomacy.

The basic mission of the Corps of Discovery was more commercial than imperialistic. "The object of your mission," directed President Thomas Jefferson, "is to explore the Missouri river, & such principal stream of it, as, by it's course and communication with the waters of the Pacific ocean . . . may offer the most direct & practical water communication across this continent for the purposes of commerce." Thus were Lewis and Clark envoys for free-trade agreements, long prior to NAFTA and CAFTA and the WTO.

Indeed, Lewis and Clark's experience revealed that, rather than an empty wilderness ripe for simple exploitation, the West was a continuous map of economic nations, intricate in culture and society, interactive and adaptive, and sophisticated in commerce.

Trade was often an exercise in free enterprise at its best. The Corps were roundly skinned at horse-trading with the Lemhi Shoshone, as Sergeant Ordway noted on August 27, 1805: "the natives do not wish to part with any more of their horses without gitting a higher price for them. The most of those he [Captain Clark] has bought as yet was for about 3 or 4 dollars worth of marchandize at the first cost, but we will have to give a little more to git a fiew more horses."[1] But they had to

1. Gary E. Moulton, *The Lewis and Clark Journals: An American Epic of Discovery.* The Abridgment of the Definitive Nebraska Edition (Lincoln: University of Nebraska Press, 2003), 199.

Two Crow Indians on horseback, around 1908.
Courtesy Edward S. Curtis Collection
(Library of Congress).

be good sports about it because the classical supply and demand curves were necessarily crossing fairly high on the graph for the time being. And time was money, or trinkets anyway.

The point to be extracted from this engaging story is that American Indians never have been strangers to the good old American entrepreneurial spirit. Lewis and Clark experienced it in spades.

And the point to be projected from here forward is that contemporary American Indian sovereignty depends directly upon a successful rekindling of that entrepreneurial spirit. It's the Indian way.

EVOLUTION OF THE POLITICAL CULTURE

In 1971 Alvin Josephy, along with a host of other leading thinkers, declared the emergence of a new paradigm for Indians: self-determination. He defined the concept as "the right of Indians to decide programs and policies for themselves, to manage their own affairs, to govern themselves, and to control their land and its resources."[2] The announcement gave structure and characterization to the policy evolution that has occupied the Indian debate for the ensuing thirty years, and progress toward that vision has been substantial.

In fact, tribal self-determination has been perfected to a concept called "Tribal Sovereignty," which has achieved the status of governmental policy and has become the everyday idiom shared by Indian and non-Indian citizenry alike. Seminal court cases have been fought and won and (equally often) lost, defining the jurisdictional boundaries around Indian tribes' prerogative of self-government. The arguments are still habitually cast in collectives of "the Indian" and "the White Man," just as the original conceptualization of "Red Power" was envisioned in Alvin Josephy's pivotal book.

Tribal Sovereignty has risen to the art of political correctness.

BEYOND TRIBAL SOVEREIGNTY

Now, having succeeded for the most part in defining "tribal self-determination" and having succeeded for certain in implanting "Tribal Sovereignty" in the national language, it is time for evolution to the next paradigm, which might well be entitled "Indian Sovereignty." There is a difference.

Huge credit is due the warriors of Tribal Sovereignty. But we must respectfully propose that this paradigm has an obvious shortcoming, indeed a glaring vulnerability, which lies in its lack of consideration and priority for the role of the Indian citizen, the individual, the person. After all, even with Tribal Sovereignty we continue to experience devastating personal and family-level despair: poverty and

2. Alvin M. Josephy, Jr., *Red Power: The American Indians' Fight for Freedom* (New York: McGraw-Hill, 1971).

unemployment twice the national average; consistently lower educational success than the national norm; alcohol-related mortality rates triple the national average.[3]

We should think of these human imperatives as matters of Indian Sovereignty, as distinct from Tribal Sovereignty. Shift to Indian-think (that is, Indian as the person) versus Tribal-think (tribal as the collective). In the long run, Indian Sovereignty—the autonomy of the Indian person—will prove to be at least equally crucial.

That is, the imperative to re-equip Indian people with the dignity of self-sufficiency, the right to not depend upon the White Man, the Government, even the Tribe.

This is not a new notion, to be sure. In fact, it is only a circling-back to the ancient and most crucial of Indian values—an understanding that the power of the tribal community is founded upon the collective energy of strong, self-sufficient, self-initiating, entrepreneurial, independent, healthful, and therefore powerful individual persons. Human beings. Indians.

EVOLVING OUR CULTURAL-ECONOMIC MYTH

Consider this for evidence: even a cursory review of our revered community archives of tradition, story, and legend reveals a recurring celebration of the man or woman who is distinguished for their empathy and generosity toward someone less fortunate. Empathy and generosity, the highest of civil values. But whence comes the capacity, the wherewithal, for generosity? Obviously, the celebrated sharer of his or her largesse had to have been resourceful and capable enough to generate their shareable wealth, however great or modest in the story, in the first place. Call it enterprise or entrepreneurship or productive capability, it is the underlying assumption of the legend. That is the Indian way. Always has been.

---

3. "Fact Sheet: Key Statistics about Native America" (Cambridge, Mass.: The Harvard Project on American Indian Economic Development), September 2004.

This is not to diminish the reality of historical (and stubborn contemporary) external forces of oppression and injustice—displacement, incarceration, forced dependency, impoverishment, and human trauma of the worst kinds. The bicentennial commemoration of the Corps of Discovery evokes bitter memories of injustice and tragedy. But Amy Mossett, Hidatsa-Mandan historian, insists that we must move on: "Our tribes have survived catastrophic events in the past 200 years. But if we grieve forever, we will never move forward."[4]

Along the line between today and the time of Lewis and Clark, something has gone awry with our proud and powerful Indian myth (using that term to mean self-actualizing identity). In fact, Indians might even have started down the path toward dependency if our ancestors swallowed the seed planted by Meriwether Lewis in his stock speech to tribal leadership, exemplified in his August 16, 1805, diary of the day's proceedings with the Lemhi Shoshone: "[W]e made them sensible of their dependance on the will of our government for every species of merchandize as well for their defence & comfort; and apprized them of the strength of our government and it's friendly disposition towards them."[5] (The spelling is his.)

In any case, a sharp and destructive dissonance has arisen between our most revered cultural standards and our operational culture, the latter being slashed by personal and community despondency—born of the loss of dignity that attends self-sufficiency. Dependency has become the reality of our daily existence.

We may as well call this what it is: a downward spiral of personal and community despair. Worst of all, generation by generation it becomes what sociologists term "learned helplessness"—an internalized sense of no personal possibility, transmitted hereditarily and reinforced by recurring circumstances of hopelessness. The ugly truth is that the manifestations are epidemic: substance abuse, violence, depression, crime, trash.

4. Margo Roosevelt, "Tribal Culture Clash," *Time*, July 8, 2002, 68.
5. Gary E. Moulton, ed., *The Definitive Journals of Lewis and Clark* (Lincoln: University of Nebraska Press, 1987), 4:111.

The powerful danger for Indians lies in capitulation to victimhood as an acceptable community myth (again, self-actualizing identity); in other words, when we Indians give in and begin to believe that we have no constructive personal prospects. Excuse-making and blame are potent narcotics that provide shelter for irresponsibility, incompetence, and failure of personal initiative.

Michael Running Wolf, Northern Cheyenne, admonishes us Indians and the community at large to beware the victimhood myth: "[W]e walk the border between protecting our values, and acting the part of victim. Not victims in the sense of being injured individuals, but subscribing to the belief that we deserve sympathy. It's a belief that bases our identity upon the wrongs we have endured, rather than our accomplishments and integrity. It's a phenomenon that demands the nurturing of victimhood."[6]

Running Wolf is right. There is no future in victimhood and its self-destructive corollaries—excuses and dependency.

We are far better off to apply our finite personal energy to a constructive belief system and a corresponding action plan. Michael Running Wolf declares the imperative philosophical base: "Empowerment not crafted by one's own strengths is an illusion."[7]

Of course, it is not enough to simply declare it so. In fact, every Indian community will have to make a determined effort to confront our realities, analyze our conditions and our prospects with all of the tools of modern social science, and then chart a strategic course back to individual and community strength. We must do it by ourselves and for ourselves, so that we will understand it, own it, and believe in it. The task of changing our paradigm will take time and tools that we can generate on our own terms.

It is time to move beyond training only teachers and lawyers and petroleum engineers, and to begin preparing some smart, energetic, and dedicated young Indian sociologists and psychologists and geographers and economists and M.B.A.'s.

6. Michael Running Wolf, letter to the editor, *Bozeman Daily Chronicle*, November 2, 2004.
7. Ibid.

"It is not Indian to fail!" Birdena Realbird, a Crow public-school educator, irrefutable traditionalist in her own right, asserts that excuse-making serves no constructive end.[8] To say that Indians cannot be expected to excel in the contemporary universe because of our Indian-ness is the worst kind of insult to the honor of our proud culture and blood heritage. Rather, argues Realbird, we ought to view ourselves as fortified by our heritage and therefore better equipped than most other folks to prevail over whatever challenge arises. Personal accomplishment follows robust expectations and vital community psychology follows both. Now, that is a myth to evolve to. Or, as we should choose to believe, to return to. That is the Indian Way as it was before Lewis and Clark.

Lewis recorded this observation on August 19, 1805, having become familiar with the Lemhi Shoshone: "they are frank, communicative, fair in dealing, generous with the little they possess, extremely honest, and by no means beggarly."[9] In spite of his Eurocentricity, Lewis could only admire the strength of character of all the tribal peoples the Corps of Discovery met. That kind of strength will sustain us today if only we will set our minds to it.

RETHINKING TRIBAL GOVERNMENT

Besides the standard roll call of culprits, sometimes even tribal government is guilty of making matters worse by advancing policies of paternalism, institutional racism, and economic dependency. At its worst, tribal politics thrives upon keeping Indian constituencies corralled, whether by fostering some form of socioeconomic dependency on tribal-government programs or plain old familial bullying. At its most benign, tribal government has failed to grasp what virtually all other institutions in the world know: government is inherently poorly suited to being in business.

8. Birdena Realbird, personal communication, 2004.
9. Gary E. Moulton, *The Definitive Journals of Lewis and Clark*, 5:119.

Indians as stockholders in the tribal enterprise, such as the tribal casino, even receiving a dividend ("per capita") from time to time (after tribal government extracts its cut off the top, just like government anywhere) is a fine enough business model—for a tribe, for the collective, the corporate. But the tribal corporate model contributes little, if anything, to the capacity of the Indian person, the individual, to be really independent and self-sufficient in any business sense. Most tribal government–sponsored economic-development efforts are locked in Tribal-think to the total exclusion of, or even in direct competition with, Indian private enterprise.

This is not to deny the crucial imperative of the tribal consciousness. After all, we are keenly aware every moment of who we are and what we are about as Indians. But it is important for purposes of this discussion to respectfully distinguish between The Tribe as traditional tribal ethic and The Tribe as functional governmental entity. Sadly, the two are too often contradictory.

Tribal Sovereignty (that phrase should be purged and replaced because it conjures up unrealistic expectations and grounds for an unnecessary fistfight all around)—that is, the prerogative of governing territory and interactions among people—is a very necessary, inherently tribal government purpose. That is why we have such a lively economy in the Indian law world, even when the rest of the regular Indians flounder in poverty.

The trouble is that we Indians (and everybody else, for that matter) are so focused on tribal-think and on the vastly entertaining matters of tribal jurisdiction, which by definition entails power, control, and influence, that we completely overlook the daily exigencies of Indian living. Secondarily and reactively, tribal governments try hard to rescue the people by "program." Typically, comparatively little of the tribal-government energy and budget ever goes to initiatives to empower people toward sustainable self-sufficiency. But Tribal Sovereignty costs lots of money and, frankly, it is much easier and terrifically sexier than those messy human issues.

It is not our intention to downgrade the necessity for the inherently governmental services of The Tribe in the functional arenas that government can do well. Let us simply insist that the proper economic role for tribal government ought to be to ensure necessary infrastructure and then facilitate private enterprise for Indian entrepreneurs, with an eye toward building the capacity of individuals and families to be truly independent.

In their paper "Sovereignty and Nation-Building: The Development Challenge in Indian Country Today," Stephen Cornell and Joseph Kalt of Harvard University point out the necessary prerequisites for sustainable entrepreneurship in Indian communities: stable institutions and policies; fair and effective dispute resolution; separation of politics from business management; a competent bureaucracy; and cultural coherence. "Tribes have had to back up their assertions of self-governance with the ability to govern effectively. It is one thing to have the power to govern; it is another to deliver effective governance."[10] Cornell and Kalt go on to assert that economic self-sufficiency is a crucial element of meaningful self-determination. And there is plenty of evidence that tribal government can make it or break it.

"The central problem," Joseph Kalt has said, "is to create an environment in which investors—whether tribal members or outsiders—feel secure, and therefore are willing to put energy, time, and capital into the tribal economy."[11]

Is it too much heresy to imagine that some of the enormous intelligence, resourcefulness and creativity ensconced in the tribal official/tribal attorney reservoir could be redirected to making this happen?

10. Stephen Cornell and Joseph P. Kalt, "Sovereignty and Nation-Building: The Development Challenge in Indian Country Today" (paper, The Harvard Project on American Indian Economic Development, 1998), 10.
11. Statement made by Joseph P. Kalt before the U.S. Senate Committee on Indian Affairs, September 17, 1996.

THE "NOT-INDIAN" FALLACY

Two standard objections are predictable. First, "it's not-Indian" to be in business. (We fall back on the not-Indian defense so often that it deserves its own hyphenation. Like, "It's not-Indian to get good grades." Or, "It's not-Indian to stray long from the rez." Or, "It's not-Indian to speak English without a rez accent.")

Sorry. We have already pointed out the historical record that Indians were certainly all about entrepreneurship when the Corps of Discovery reported the scene, first among each other and then in commercial engagement with the emerging French, English, Spanish and finally American business potentials. To be sure, the practical aftermath of the Lewis and Clark visitation was the steady erosion of Indians' economic autonomy, including explicit federal policy to eradicate the last vestiges of the customary economic base, the bison. With neither opportunity, means, or encouragement, it is no surprise that the entrepreneurial spirit has faded over many generations.

But to dismiss entrepreneurship as inherently not-Indian is simply mistaken. Indeed, that would guarantee self-defeat in the context of a global socio-political-economic milieu that is driven by profit. Furthermore, we all know a few hardy Indian souls who are making it on their own. Perhaps the buffalo and beaver are gone, but we Indians are nothing if not durable, adaptable, and creative, and we had better apply those qualities to new forms of economy. The Great White Father has been our buffalo for 150 years now, but we have a hunch that that, too, may vanish someday, equally unceremoniously. We would do well to be ahead of the game.

Not yet persuaded, some will turn to the second standard objection: that individual enterprise contradicts our Indian sense of and commitment to the welfare of the whole, the tribe.

Of course, our ancient ethic of the interdependence of all people and all things is one of the gifts that we Indians have to offer Western

European-American philosophy whenever our neighbors are at last willing to acknowledge it. We treasure that sense of kinship and community that has always been key to our survival.

With all due respect, however, we have already recognized the corollary truth that the wherewithal for generosity and sharing must, by definition, originate in some initiative, enterprise, and creativity on somebody's part. That is neither selfish nor greedy; it is simply being resourceful and capable, perhaps even motivated by a desire to be altruistic and generous with the product of one's work.

"You've got to take care of yourself, and then you can take care of your family and your community," says Shane Doyle, a smart young graduate student and a singer from a traditional Crow family.[12] There is not an inherent contradiction in that truth. But to buy into the opposite thinking is to kill personal motivation and, ultimately, buy back into the deadly dynamics that got us in this fix in the first place. We know in our guts that the strength of our community depends upon the strength and capability of every person that constitutes it. That is no less true now than it was in 1806, our pivot point for this conversation.

SEIZING OUR DESTINY

What endures, and shall always sustain us if we choose to pursue it, is our strength, our uniqueness, our confidence as Indians. Within that framework of profound spiritual commitment, our cultures have always evolved on a multitude of fronts—religious, material, linguistic, economic, artistic, intellectual. To remain viable, we have perpetually adapted our cultures to changing times, conditions, and influences, usually favorably, sometimes disastrously. These days, and perhaps it has always been thus, we agonize individually and as communities and tribes about selecting our evolutionary options. Too often, we find it tempting to time-freeze our myth (that is, our

12. Shane Doyle, personal communication, 2004.

sense of who we are and how we are to fit in the universe), usually in an era already past, and then enforce it with a posse of culture police. We have a sense of foreboding, however, as we feel the cognitive dissonance between our daily operational culture and our traditional culture, which increasingly is reserved for periodic celebrations. We cannot afford to allow that gap to become irreconcilable.

But we are pragmatic, too, and by some inscrutable process of cultural consensus we continue to adapt. Instinctively we anticipate the inevitability of cultural termination if we do not always allow our culture to be relevant to and within our daily, operational lives.

Indian communities must be visionary enough, wise enough as we always have been, to give our people permission to evolve our culture so that it is relevant in our personal existence.

A linchpin to all of this is economic security on a purely personal Indian basis. We don't need much, but we cannot function in today's world without some semblance of economic dignity. If we can achieve that, then we can free our creative energies for the greater works of community vitality and Tribal Sovereignty. Accordingly, we must give Indians permission to pursue that age-old but now-remembered paradigm of entrepreneurial self-sufficiency. Surely that is not all of a solution, but at least it is part of the puzzle.

We trust that if we empower our people to seize their own Indian destinies then they will take care of our tribal destiny. That is the Indian way.

IF THE CORPS HAD DISCOVERED THE CROWS

Clark was righteously sore about his loss of valuable horses, ostensibly to some nocturnal Crow Indian entrepreneurs. He vented his pique by actually drafting an extensive speech by means of which he would chastise the Crows. "Children. Your Great Father will be very sorry to hear of the (Crows) stealing the horses of his Chiefs warrors whome he sent out to do good to his red children on the waters of the Missoure." But then he goes on magnanimously: "Children. If any one two or 3 or your great chiefs wishes to visit your great father and go with me . . . You will then see with your own eyes and here with your own years what the white people can do for you. They do not speak with two tongues nor promis what they can't perform."[13]

We can only wonder how the Crows would have reacted, had Clark ever found them to deliver his diatribe.

It is not so hard to imagine how we would respond to that speech today.

Probably we would say: Meriwether and Billy. Welcome back after all these years. Bring horses.

13. Landon Y. Jones, *William Clark and the Shaping of the West* (New York: Hill and Wang, 2004), 144–45.

OUR PEOPLE HAVE ALWAYS BEEN HERE

Roberta Conner

ROBERTA CONNER—Sisaawipam—is Cayuse, Umatilla, and Nez Perce in heritage and a member of the Confederated Tribes of the Umatilla Indian Reservation. Known familiarly as "Bobbie," Ms. Conner has been an ardent representative of her people and of all Indians since her high school days in Pendleton, Oregon. After obtaining a journalism degree at the University of Oregon and a master's in management from Willamette University, Bobbie opted for the public sector, including an early five-year spell at an Indian foundation providing technical assistance to federal Indian-educational programs in the Northwest. In 1984 she was named a Presidential Management intern and moved along in federal service, ultimately to head up the Sacramento district of the U.S. Small Business Administration.

In the late 1990s Ms. Conner decided to come home, and in April 1998 took over as director of the Tamástslikt Cultural Institute of the Confederated Tribes of the Umatilla Indian Reservation. The Institute opened in August 1998 with a threefold mission—to preserve the three tribes' cultures, to present accurately the tribes' history, and to contribute to the development of a tribal economy.

In the years since beginning her directorship, Bobbie Conner has lectured, written, and traveled extensively in support of that mission, while at the same time fulfilling an important role in a wide range of public activities of concern to Indians and non-Indians alike. Closer to the project at hand, Bobbie is vice president of the National Council of the Lewis and Clark Bicentennial Board of Directors and a member of its Circle of Tribal Advisors.

OUR PEOPLE HAVE ALWAYS
BEEN HERE

Kwáalisim Púucha Chná Naami Natítayt (Walla Walla)
Táaminwa Pawachá Chná Naami Tanánma (Umatilla)

INTRODUCTION

To hear tribal history requires listening to many connected stories—all interrelated, just as all things in creation are connected. Looking back at our tribes' recent past, the arrival of Lewis and Clark and company is part of the same story as that of subsequent arrivals—other explorers, then trappers and traders, then emigrants—which led to the Treaty of 1855 and the tribes' move to the reservation. These are not events unique unto themselves. They are connected to ancient times and modern times because they shape the stories of our people, who are still here, and the stories of our lands on which we still live. Lewis and Clark are also connected to subsequent incursions by the Founding Fathers' visions of a continental nation and the consistency of methods used to obtain lands and to justify the taking of them from native peoples, reaching back to the 1400s.

If each person's life is a story, then the lives of Lewis and Clark and the Indians who received them are not only the story of the time of the expedition. In one lifetime much would change. Men who were little boys at the time of the expedition's arrival would, forty-nine years and seven months later, be asked to cede their homeland to Lewis and Clark's "great chief," albeit the man in the presidential chair had changed. One tribal leader would argue in 1855 that they had been good to Lewis and Clark but that they had been blind. In Clark's next career as superintendent of Indian Affairs for the Missouri Territory, he would use the relationships he made with some tribes during the expedition in order to move them to what is now Oklahoma. Each story unfolds to the next story. They are not isolated.

And yet, in the Lewis and Clark bicentennial years starting in 2003, the focus of non-Indians resides in the three-year journey of exploration and all that was recorded along the route of the search for the fabled Northwest Passage. Visitors to our museum on the Umatilla Reservation want to hear about two weeks two hundred years ago—the snapshot of time when the expedition was in our homeland. This tunnel vision results from seeing the expedition as a lone event, one moment in time, rather than the larger act of premeditated expansionism that was embedded in the historical context. Our typical visitor considers the popular notion of exploration as the goal for the great journey and nothing more. It is more; it is the first incursion and the beginning of the invasion in the Columbia River Plateau. It is the advent of dispossession for our tribes. It is the intentional extension of the European form of colonization into the Pacific Northwest. It is the fulfillment of the prophecy that our tribal lives would change and that we would need to endure great difficulty to survive. And survive we have. Against all odds, our people are still in their homeland, and like many other tribes, working to rebuild their nations—like the phoenix from the ashes. We want to tell the whole story right up to today, and we want our fellow Americans to hear it.

We are descendants of the people described in the journals, and we still live in much the same area as we did when the expedition traversed our homeland in 1805 and again in 1806. The Walla Walla, Umatilla, and Cayuse Tribes, as we are now known, make up the Confederated Tribes of the Umatilla Indian Reservation just east of Pendleton, Oregon. The population of our Confederacy is about 2,470 enrolled members, growing from our lowest numbers near 1,100 in the 1880s, yet still well below the estimated 8,000 at time of contact. Tribes with whom we are linguistically and culturally related include the Warm Springs, Wanapum, Palouse, Yakama, and Nez Perce. Our people have always been here. We intend to be here—in the place the Creator gave us to live—forever.

OUR WAY OF LIFE

OCTOBER 19, 1805   . . . *The great chief Yel-lep-pit two other chiefs, and a Chief of Band below presented themselves to us verry early this morning. we Smoked with them, enformed them as we had all others above as well as we Could by Signs of our friendly intentions towards our red children Perticular those who opened their ears to our Councils . . . Seven lodges of Indians drying fish, at our approach they hid themselves in their Lodges and not one was to be seen untill we passed . . . while Setting on a rock wateing for Capt Lewis I Shot a Crain which was flying over of the common kind. I observed a great number of Lodges . . . others I Saw . . . delayed but a Short time before they returned to their Lodges as fast as they could run . . . the enteranc or Dores of the Lodges wer Shut with . . . a mat, I approached one with a pipe in my hand entered a lodge . . . found 32 persons . . . Some crying and ringing there hands, others hanging their heads . . . They said we came from the clouds . . . and were not men &c &c.*

WILLIAM CLARK

This place in the Columbia River Plateau is our home. Our people have always been here in what are now northeastern Oregon and southeastern Washington. How long is always? As far back as our oral histories recall. Back to when the landforms were created, back to the end of the cold times, back to the floods, back to the times when the mountains hurled rocks and fire at each other, back to when the animals held council and taught us how to live here. Our covenants on how to exist in this homeland are ancient. From the animals, plants, waterways, and the cycles provided by the seasons, we learned what to eat, where to live at different times of the year, how to heal ourselves and take care of one another. Our traditional laws, still in place, never replaced or superceded, tell us how to take care of the gifts from the Creator. In our cultures, children are sacred as are all the beings made by the Creator. That is the age-old context into which Lewis and Clark arrived in 1805. By virtue of their saying so, these newcomers proclaimed we were children to their Great Father. Not so. We were and are children of this landscape that sustains us and upon which we have depended for eons. They did not speak our languages. They shot a crane flying by for no reason apparent to onlookers. They entered a closed door without seeking permission. Then, Clark writes that we said, undoubtedly by way of signs, they came from the clouds and are other than men—godlike? Perhaps Clark's own sense of superiority and dominance has run away with his imagination.

16TH OCT. 1805   . . . *they have pleanty of beeds Copper & brass trinkets, about them which they Sign to us that they got them from Some tradors on a River to the North of this place—*

17TH OCT. 1805   . . . *a number of the Savages have red and blew cloth, but no buffalow Robes among them.*

20TH OCT. 1805   . . . *we halted at a village to dine where we bought a fiew roots &C. and Saw among them a number of articles which came from white people. Such as copper kittles Scarlet &C.*

26TH OF APRIL 1806   . . . *a number of the natives followed us who are mooveing up the river & Some of them are going over the rockey mountn. to kill buffaloe.*

JOHN ORDWAY

Our Walla Walla, Cayuse, and Umatilla ancestors conducted trade for millennia with neighboring tribes traveling by canoe up and down the Columbia and on foot, and for centuries across the Rockies and elsewhere well beyond our homeland by horseback. The extensive trade network supplied ample opportunities to incorporate goods and concepts from other cultures and landscapes. When Lewis and Clark and the Corps of Northwestern Discovery arrived in our homeland in October of 1805, our people had lived in this place for thousands of years, had intertribal trade alliances, reciprocity agreements for safe passage, and we had conducted multi-tribal expeditions to distant lands. We had white men's goods in the mid-Columbia Plateau, evidence of our network, which Lewis and Clark documented.

APRIL 28TH 1806   . . . *being anxious to depart we requested the Cheif to furnish us with canoes to pass the river, but he insisted on our remaining with him this day at least, that he would be much pleased if we could conse[n]t to remain two or three, but he would not let us have canoes to leave him today . . . we urged the necessity of our going on immediately in order that we might the sooner return to them with the articles which they wished but this had no effect, he said that the time he asked could not make any considerable difference. I at length urged that there was no wind blowing and that the river was consequently in good order to pass our horses and if he would furnish us with canoes for that purpose we would remain all night at our present encampment, to this proposition he assented and soon produced us a couple of canoes by means of which we passed our horses over the river safely and hubbled them as usual.*

MERIWETHER LEWIS

29TH OF APRIL 1806   . . . *they have lately been at war with the Snake nation and many of them were kild.*

JOHN ORDWAY

Our ancestors controlled what happened in our homeland. By 1805, more than thirty ships had reached the coast of what is now the Pacific Northwest. But when the Lewis and Clark expedition traveled through the mid–Columbia Plateau, this land was ours. None but our people lived here. This was not part of the young United States. While Russia, Spain, France, Britain, and the United States imagined the potential of economic control over abundant resources and trade with western tribes that would follow exploration, they had no influence here. Protected by the Rocky Mountains to the east, the Blue Mountains to the south, and the Cascades to the west as well as the Columbia River narrows and falls, only native peoples lived here. We traded for white men's goods, we knew of them through our travels, and our prophecies foretold their arrival. But our local way of life was not threatened by their passage through our homeland. Thirty-three travelers were a curiosity, a trade opportunity.

14TH OCT. 1805 . . . *the canoe I had charge of ran fast on a rock in the middle of the river and turned across the rock. we attempeted to git hir off but the waves dashed over hir So that She filled with water. we held hir untill one of the other canoes was unloaded and came to our assistance considerable of the baggage washed overboard, but the most of it was taken up below when the canoe got lightned She went of[f] of a sudden & left myself and three more Standing on the rock half leg deep in the rapid water untill a canoe came to our assistance. we got the most of the baggage to Shore two mens bedding lost one tommahawk, and some other Small articles a Small copper kittle &C.*

JOHN ORDWAY

The expedition was in our country when they came here; they were beyond the boundary of the United States, beyond the Louisiana Purchase. Our customs, our languages, our diet, our housing, our clothing, and our laws all emanated from the landscape that cared for us. The expedition traveled through, much as any travelers would, taking in as much as possible, learning what they could aided by the Nez Perce men who accompanied them here, and making assumptions. They were foreigners in our land, but in the journals, they write of things foreign or new to them. It is no wonder that some errors of misunderstanding or of omission occurred. One oral history of our people recounts how the explorers, and there were many after Lewis and Clark, were generally poor housekeepers and existed precariously among us, making it evident they did not belong here. Our ancestors hoped they would get home where they belonged.

Lewis and Clark were renaming rather than naming rivers "Lewis's," "Drewyer's," or "LePage's" rivers while passing through. They also renamed peoples in making their records. The peoples Lewis and Clark called Wallahwollah call themselves Waluulapam.

A tule mat Umatilla lodge. Image courtesy of
Special Collections and University Archives,
University of Oregon libraries.

"Walla Walla" describes the many small flows of water that braid their way to the main stem of the Columbia River in that area. More than likely, their two Nez Perce escorts informed the expedition of the name of the waterway and then the expedition applied that name to the people. And the name stuck. Subsequent travelers referred to the people the same way. Walla Walla is how the tribe was referred to in the treaty of 1855 and is to this day. To native peoples then and now, each landmark and waterway has an ancient story that, when abbreviated, was represented by a name or title for that place. These names are still here, that is, as long as we retain and per-petuate that knowledge carried in indigenous languages. Today, the Cayuse language is extinct, save for about four hundred docu-mented words, and most Cayuse descendants who speak a native language speak lower or upper Nez Perce. The few persons who speak Walla Walla as a first language are all elders. Those who speak Umatilla as a first language are a handful of adults and a few elders.

Lewis and Clark heard at least three languages on October 16, 1805, at the confluence of the Snake and Columbia rivers. That they did not know precisely which ones, or did not have the time to find out, is not important. What is important is the knowledge that is embedded in our tribal languages that accurately and efficiently tells the history of the ecosystems of the Columbia River drainage system.

In his second inaugural address on March 4, 1805, President Jefferson observed:

> These persons inculcate a sanctimonious reverence for the customs of their ancestors; that whatsoever they did, must be done through all time; that reason is a false guide, and to advance under its counsel, in their physical, moral, or political condition, is perilous innovation; that their duty is to remain as their Creator made them, ignorance being safety, and knowledge full of danger . . .

Today, our people persist in resembling the observation regarding our sanctimonious reverence for the customs of our ancestors. It would be unwise to do otherwise. After thousands of years on this landscape, their empirical knowledge should be revered. This reverence for the ancient covenant between our people and salmon, for example, resulted in the ethic that one should never take all of anything in harvest. Always leave some fish to pass upriver, roots and berries for the other species who eat them. This same ancient covenant led the modern Confederated Tribes of Umatilla to undertake extraordinary efforts to successfully restore water flows and salmon to the Umatilla and Walla Walla rivers.

OCTOBER 18, 1805 . . . *late at night the Chief came down accompanied by 20 men, and formed a Camp a Short distance above, the chief brought with him a large basket of mashed berries which he left at our Lodge as a present.*

WILLIAM CLARK

APRIL 27TH 1806 . . . *This Village consists of 15 large mat lodges . . . Yellept harranged his village in our favour intreated them to furnish us with fuel and provision and set the example himself by bringing us an armfull of wood and a platter of 3 roasted mullets. the others soon followed his example with rispect to fuel and we soon found ourselves in possession of an ample stock . . . they also informed us, that there were a plenty of deer and Antelopes on the road, with good water and grass.*

MERIWETHER LEWIS

Abundance is the standard in our culture, rather than scarcity. Our tribal characteristics emanated from our extended families, our close-knit village lives, our language groups, and our environment. Lewis and Clark described the Walla Walla as "the most hospitable, honest, sincere people that we have met with in our voyage." These complimentary journal entries describe virtues and values that directly reflected our culture, wherein people were well provided for by the landscape and their own industry. Our leaders were accus-

An Umatilla lodge and women drying eels on racks.
Image courtesy of Special Collections and University Archives,
University of Oregon libraries.

tomed to housing and feeding large gatherings. Efficient and effective food preparation, preservation, and storage methods sustained us year round, and our architecture was reliant on easily renewable resources. The journals comprehensively document our fishing practices, our numerous tule mat–lodge villages, the variety of roots we harvested, and our vast horse herds. We did not live in scarcity. We had learned through the ages to be prepared to care for others, including visitors from distant places.

OCTOBER 19TH 1805   *. . . those Lodges can turn out <250>350 men . . . opposite 24 Lodges of Indians . . . about 100 Inds. come over . . .*

WILLIAM CLARK

Our homeland was neither an unoccupied frontier nor a wilderness. In fact, the concept of wilderness does not directly translate into our languages because it is a foreign construct. The Corps' journey from what is now North Dakota to what is now Oregon included contact with many tribal peoples. When the expedition arrived in the Columbia River Plateau, they entered one of the most populous areas they had been in since leaving the Mandan villages. And the Mandan villages, despite decimation by disease, were more densely populated than St. Louis, then a western outpost. The Corps of Discovery's "western estimate of Indians" included 114 tribes that are now represented by at least 58 modern tribal nations. Their estimate, while incomplete, included about 117 lodges and 4,700 estimated "soles" that were ancestors to the tribes now in our confederation of Cayuse, Umatilla, and Walla Walla.

OCTOBER 19TH SATURDAY 1805   *The great chief Yel-lep-pit two other chiefs, and a Chief of Band below presented themselves to us verry early this morning . . . Yelleppit is a bold handsom Indian, with a dignified countenance about 35 years of age, about 5 feet 8 inches high and well perpotiond. he requested us to delay untill the Middle of the day, that his people might Come down and See us, we excused our Selves and promised to Stay with him one*

or 2 days on our return which appeared to Satisfy him; great numbers of Indi-
ans Came down in Canoes to view us before we Set out . . .

WILLIAM CLARK

Lewis and Clark were an attraction when they arrived in our
homeland in 1805. One of our leaders twice entreats them to stay
longer so that more of his people may come and see them. One
of our elders tells this history: "When the first people came to
Umatilla, they had a colored man with them. And the kids got
scared. They thought he was like a monster or something. The kids
really behaved themselves. . . ." Another elder was told that her
ancestors had found the men of the expedition peculiar because
they appeared to be eating themselves—the men would reach
into their breeches and pull something out to eat. They had pock-
ets in their leggings or pants, which our people did not have in
theirs. That people came by the hundreds to view the expedition
members is evidence of the effectiveness of the moccasin tele-
graph and suggests just how peculiar and novel these travelers
were.

20TH OF APRIL 1806   *. . . all the Indians we have Seen play a game & risque*
all the property they have at different games. the game that these Savages play
is by setting in a circle & have a Small Smooth bone in their hands & Sing
crossing their hands to fix it in a hidden manner from the other Side who gass
the hand that has it in then counts one a Stick Stuck in the ground for the tal-
lies & So on untill one Side or the other wins the property Stacked up. this
game is played with activity, and they appear merry & peaceable. Capt. Lewis
took the property from the man that gambled away our horse. . . . the Indians
would not give us any thing worth mentioning for our canoes So we Split &
burnt one of them this evening.

JOHN ORDWAY

Various games and forms of gambling have been used for centuries, if not longer, to redistribute wealth along the Columbia River.

Lewis and Clark apparently wanted to engage in trade straightaway but did not wish to use their canoe to gamble for what they might obtain in a more time-consuming and chancy manner. But one of the men of the expedition did take a turn and lost a horse and then lost the gains from gambling to the captain. That gambling is inappropriate in any way is not our cultural conclusion. That judgment arrives with missionaries. In today's world, roughly 40 percent of federally recognized tribes use gaming as a means to an end. Without the benefit of a significant tax base to fund essential government services, tribes use the net profits from gaming to provide fire, police, sanitation, and emergency medical services as well as education and youth and elder care, among other necessities. Gaming also provides jobs and incomes on reservations where unemployment previously stagnated for decades between 40 and 80 percent.

APRIL 28TH 1806 . . . *we found a Shoshone woman, prisoner among these people by means of whome and Sahcahgarweah we found the means of conversing with the Wollah-wollahs* . . .

MERIWETHER LEWIS

Modern-day Umatillas playing the traditional hand game.
Photograph courtesy of the Tamastslikt Cultural Institute.

APRIL 28TH 1806   *This morning early the Great Chief Yel lip pet brought a very eligant white horse to our Camp and presented him to me Signifying his wish to get a kittle but being informed that we had already disposed of every kittle we could possibly Spare he Said he was Content with what ever I thought proper to give him. I gave him my Swoard, 100 balls & powder and Some Small articles of which he appeared perfectly Satisfied* . . .

WILLIAM CLARK

APRIL 29TH 1806   *We gave Small Medals to two inferior Chiefs of this nation, and they each furnished us with a fine horse, in return we gave them Sundery articles among which was one of Capt Lewis's Pistols & Several hundred rounds of Amunition.*

WILLIAM CLARK

Tribal practices included taking captives during raids on neighboring rivals. The captive or slave station in the family and community was not necessarily permanent. A captive could ascend to higher stature by excelling, demonstrating worth to the community, and proving commitment to the people. York, for example, given his skills and record of service to Clark, would likely have fared better amongst Indians. For us, raids were a means of obtaining goods, livestock, and productive labor from those with whom we did not routinely trade. Raids and warfare were not conducted for the purpose of annihilation of another people. It would be counterproductive to completely eliminate another people. Clark, alternatively, indicates in his October 19, 1805, field notes about his encounter with the Umatillas that "Indians [were] much fritened . . . I am confident I could have tomahawked every Indian here." While the statement is innocuous enough, it provides an important glimpse into the psyche of Clark, who is leading an advance party, with the rest of the Corps following at some distance. For a moment Clark feels no vulnerability, and he is aware of that. Perhaps even more telling are the trades that Lewis and Clark conduct upon their return in April 1806.

Whether it is out of confidence from being amicably greeted and well hosted by the Walla Wallas or out of the paucity and recklessness that were more common on their return journey is unclear, but one of our ancestors received Clark's sword, one hundred balls, and powder. Another received one of Lewis's pistols and several hundred rounds of ammunition. Evidently, the leaders of the expedition did not fear for their lives among our people, or were too long too far from home to be careful.

OCTOBER 17TH 1805   ... *This river is remarkably Clear and Crouded with Salmon in maney places, I observe in assending great numbers of Salmon dead on the Shores, floating on the water and in the Bottoms which can be seen at the debth of 20 feet. the Cause of the emence numbers of dead Salmon I can't account for So it is I must have seen 3 or 400 dead and maney living* ...

WILLIAM CLARK

OCTOBER 18, 1805   ... *great numbers of Indians appeared to be on this Island, and emence quantities of fish Scaffold ... on the Stard. Side is 2 Lodges of Indians Drying fish, ... passed an Island Close under the Stard. Side on which was 2 Lodges of Indians drying fish on Scaffolds as above ... on this Island is two Lodges of Indians, drying fish, on the fourth Island Close under the Stard. Side is nine large Lodges of Indians Drying fish on Scaffolds as above* ...

WILLIAM CLARK

APRIL 29TH   ... *thought it best to remain on the Wallah Wallah river about a mile from the Columbia untill the morning, accordingly encamped on that river near a fish Wear ... they have also a Small Seine managed by one person, it bags in the manner of the Scooping nets ... there are 12 other Lodges of the Wallahwallah Nation on this river a Short distance below our Camp. those as well as those beyond the Columbia appear to depend on their fishing weres for their Subsistance* ...

WILLIAM CLARK

We were resident; Lewis and Clark and all members of the expedition were transient. They saw much that they did not comprehend, even when they tried in earnest to understand. In fact, as they traveled in service to President Jefferson's expansionist fantasy of seeking a direct water route through the continent, they were exploring the place the Creator gave us in which to live. The Creator gave everyone a place to live. Why were they in our country, living precariously in a place they did not belong? Moreover, why would our ancestors be so hospitable to these strangers? Why not? They were thirty-three travelers merely passing through, who did not represent a threat to our way of life at the time of their passing and for years to come. Could anyone foresee that, 109 years later, dams on the Umatilla River would prevent fish passage and that our tribes would have to work for years to return water to the riverbed and reintroduce salmon to the Umatilla River after an absence of 70 years? Did anyone envision that, 152 years later, the richest salmon fishery in the West, the magnificent Celilo Falls, would be submerged under the backwaters of the Dalles Dam? That Lewis and Clark were unfamiliar with the anadromous fish teeming in the rivers—fresh with just as many spawned out lying dead—is not important. What is important is our modern challenge to protect water flows and salmon habitat and restore salmon runs not to 1950s pre-dam levels, but to the levels that Lewis and Clark indubitably witnessed.

APRIL 28TH 1806   . . . *a little before Sun Set the Chim nah poms arrived . . . they joined the Wallah wallahs . . . and formed a half circle arround our camp . . . the whole assemblage of Indians about 350 men women and Children Sung and danced at the Same time. most of them danced in the Same place they Stood and mearly jumped up to the time of their musick. Some of the men who were esteemed most brave entered the Space around which the main body were formed in Solid Column and danced in a Circular manner Side wise. at 10 P M. the dance ended and the nativs retired; they were much gratified in Seeing Some of our Party join them in their dance. one of their party who made himself the most Conspicious Charecter in the dance and Songs, we were told was a Medesene man & Could foretell things. that he had told of our Comeing into their Country and was now about to consult his God the moon if what we Said was the truth &c. &c.*

WILLIAM CLARK

We had philosophy, laws, order, and religion; we were not uncivilized or wild. We lived according to our laws in the order established in our homes and homeland. Our law emanated from our ecosystem and our philosophy and is celebrated in our music. On the night of April 28, 1806, the members of the expedition did not distinguish the kinds of songs and dances they witnessed. As native people read what some of the Corps wrote about the occasion, they recognize that the writers are describing a worship service in which each song is a prayer and they are participating in a ceremony in which the fulfillment of the prophecy of the new people coming is proclaimed. It is a Washat service. Our people still sing the prayer songs that were likely sung that night. In our longhouses, people still mark time to the prayer songs and dance jumping in time to the music in a circular, sideways manner as described two hundred years ago. Elders here have spoken of the announcement of the fulfillment of the prophecy. That Clark thought the medicine man was consulting the moon is not far from the erroneous notion assumed by the traders who later occupied Fort Nez Perce at Wallula—that we were sun worshipers. In actuality, the practice of greeting the day in prayer at sunrise, facing east, led to the traders' conclusion but we worship the Creator, the supreme light of the world, maker of all, in all our prayers.

APRIL 26TH 1806   *. . . we were over taken to day by Several families of the natius who were traveling up the river with a Numr. of horses; they Continued with us much to our ennoyance as the day was worm the roads dusty and we Could not prevent their horses Crouding in and breaking our order of March without useing Some acts of Severty which we did not wish to Commit.*

WILLIAM CLARK

APRIL 30TH 1806   . . . *this stream is a branch of the Wallahwollah river into which it discharges itself about six miles above the junction of that river with the Columbia . . . it appears to be navigable for canoes; it is deep and has a bold current . . .*

MERIWETHER LEWIS

Although our once-great horse culture is now a remnant of what it was, it is not gone. After our homeland became a "fur desert," as otter and beaver were obliterated for a hat craze in "civilized" nations, horses were our stock-in-trade. Our selective-breeding practices yielded fast, hearty horses renowned for their stamina and soundness. A few of our famously sturdy, fast equines went to Bora Bora during World War II. By the 1950s, the businesses of farming, ranching, and railroads find horses a nuisance, and the advent of post-Depression economics and the auto result in thousands of horses being "canned" for dog food and glue. Nonetheless, within our modern tribes are people who rodeo, race horses, rope, trail-ride, teach horsemanship; cut, rein, and round up cattle; and hunt on horseback. Canoe making has ceased but threatens resurgence because other neighboring tribes have maintained this skill. Many of the tribal technologies that sustained our people for millennia continue because they are valuable not as quaint traditions, but as knowledge of our universe. Hunting, fish harvest, root digging, and associated processing technologies represent ways of perpetuating the sacred species given to us on our land. Formal rites of passage for first kill, first fish, first digging, and first picking are still observed in families and in the longhouse. The ways of knowing are as valued as the land and animals that taught our ancestors. Being instructed formally and finding answers from nature are both accepted methods of obtaining knowledge.

APRIL 30TH 1806   . . . *this plain as usual is covered with arromatic shrubs hurbatious plants and a short grass. many of those plants produce those esculent roots which form a principal part of the subsistence of the natives. among others there is one which produces a root somewhat like the sweet pit-taitoe . . . Drewyer killed a beaver and an otter; a part of the former we reserved for ourselves and gave the indians the ballance. these people will not eat the dog but feast heartily on the otter which is vastly inferior in my estima-tion, they sometimes also eat their horses, this indeed is common to all the indians who possess this annimal in the plains of Columbia; but it is only done when necessity compells them.—*

MERIWETHER LEWIS

Our indigenous diet was lean, rich, and diverse, and our people were physically active and athletic (characteristics that become espe-cially significant when compared to today's diabetes-inducing nutri-tion and lifestyles). Despite their awareness of native plant foods, members of the expedition ate, according to scholarly estimates, nine pounds of meat per man per day. If they found Indian customs pecu-liar and our diet distasteful, imagine what we thought of theirs. While we did not consume dogs, and would only consume horse meat in a rare circumstance, the Corps members preferred these meats to salmon. They bought at least fifty dogs from our camps on the out-bound journey. There was no alcohol in our diet. Unlike the expedi-tion group, we did not make spirits out of rotting camas roots. And, for regular cleansing, both physical and spiritual, we had our sweat houses and bathed frequently in streams and rivers, while the mem-bers of the expedition were smelly, according to tribal oral history.

1ST DAY OF MAY 1806   *. . . some time after we had encamped three young men arived from the Wallahwollah village bringing with them a steel trap belonging to one of our party which had been neglegently left behind; this is an act of integrity rarely witnessed among indians. during our stay with them they several times found knives of the men which had been carelessly lossed by them and returned them. I think we can justly affirm to the honor of these people that they are the most hospitable, honest, and sincere people that we have met with in our voyage.—*

MERIWETHER LEWIS

Native peoples were not heathens, thieves, squaw drudges, savages, or even chiefs. While Indians were described as such in the journals of the six men in the expedition who could write, these were all terms given to us by others outside our cultures that represented common vernacular of the day, albeit largely derogatory. If saying it doesn't make it so, writing it down did not improve the veracity of such labels. When our Nimíipu (Nez Perce) relatives escorted them into the mid–Columbia Plateau, the explorers encountered orderly division of labor between genders, picketed graves and burial islands, veneration of elders that was obvious even to outsiders, people unafraid of new commerce opportunities, people who were multilingual, and displays of tremendous hospitality. Our people continue to be welcoming, straightforward, and heartfelt in our endeavors, and, sadly, racial epithets and derogatory labels persist.

INNOCENT JOURNEY OR RECONNAISSANCE FOR AN EMPIRE?

Our tribes were sovereign nations when President Jefferson dispatched the expedition. We were nations at the Walla Walla Treaty Council in 1855. We are nations today. Lewis and Clark carried the message of U.S. sovereignty to each of the tribal nations they met; diplomacy was part of their directive. During the face-to-face diplomatic overtures of the expedition, no one deliberated our ownership, our occupancy, or our authority. Lewis and Clark had no doubt that they were visitors. But in the "seventeen great nations" on the other coast, and across the Atlantic waters in Europe, unmistakable precedents had already shaped what would become our destiny— Manifest Destiny born of the rights of discovery.

President Jefferson expected the expedition to be thorough in their reconnaissance, documentation, and ritual enactment, and wrote very explicit instructions in his June 20, 1803, missive to Captain Lewis:

The commerce which may be carried on with the people inhabiting the line you will pursue, renders a knolege of these people important. You will therefore endeavor to make yourself acquainted, as far as diligent pursuit of your journey shall admit, with the names of the nations & their numbers; the extent & limits of their possessions; their relations with other tribes or nations; their language, traditions, monuments; their ordinary occupations in agriculture, fishing, hunting, war arts, & the implements for these; their food, clothing, & domestic accommodations; the diseases prevalent among them, & the remedies they use; moral and physical circumstance which distinguish them from the tribes they know; peculiarities in their laws, customs & dispositions; and articles of commerce they may need or furnish & to what extent . . . it will be useful to acquire what knolege you can of the state of morality, religion & information among them, as it may better enable those who endeavor to civilize & instruct them, to adapt their measures to the existing notions & practises of those on whom they are to operate. . . . In all your intercourse with the natives treat them in the most friendly & conciliatory manner which their own conduct will admit; allay all jealousies as to the object of your journey, satisfy them of it's innocence, make them acquainted with the position, extent, character, peaceable & commercial dispositions of the U.S., of our wish to be neighborly, friendly & useful to them, & of our dispositions to a commercial intercourse with them. . . . *[emphasis mine] Carry with you some matter of the kine-pox, inform those of them with whom you may be of it's efficacy as a preservative from the small pox; and instruct them & encourage them in the use of it. This may be especially done wherever you may winter.*

Lewis and Clark were not making an innocent journey of discovery into our lands. The word *discover,* according to Webster's dictionary, "presupposes exploration, investigation or chance encounter and always implies the previous existence of what becomes known."

So to discover tribes takes nothing away from our history, or so it seems, but for indigenous peoples the act of discovery is loaded, charged, and offensive. Why? Because there is a larger, more consequential, insidious application when lands and indigenous peoples are "discovered." The idea that an official government-ordered expedition of discovery conducted by a military unit is or was altruistic, innocent, virtuous, and heroic must come from the discoverer's vantage point. Such a notion is naïve, or disingenuous and reckless. The moniker of "discovery" tied to the expedition is commonly seen in terms of the group's naturalist findings and their identification of numerous waterways and peoples. The bigger picture reveals that "discovery" and the exercise of "discoverer's rights" were practices made common by European nations in their colonizing forays throughout the world; they were employed in the United States, as reflected in Jefferson's directives to Lewis and Clark; and finally, they inform the actions of Lewis and Clark.

Was there a grand design in the act of exploration carried out by Lewis and Clark? Further, if members of the expedition knowingly conducted reconnaissance with foresight and intent to dispossess Indians of their lands, should Americans still applaud their journey? Finally, should enlightenment about past injustices and pursuit of justice be goals for future generations of non-Indian as well as Indian citizens, leaders, and officials?

"[T]he dispatch of the Lewis and Clark expedition was an act of imperial policy," wrote Bernard DeVoto in *The Course of Empire*. "The United States had embarked on the path of building a transcontinental empire" and the expedition "dramatically enhanced the United States' 'discovery rights' to what became known as the Oregon Country," Stephen Dow Beckham explains in *Lewis & Clark: From the Rockies to the Pacific*. In *Founding Brothers: The Revolution-*

ary Generation, Joseph J. Ellis identifies a fully continental vision of an American empire in General Washington's 1783 annual message to the states. James P. Ronda, in *Finding the West: Explorations with Lewis and Clark,* observes that Jefferson's vision "made empire not only possible, but somehow almost predetermined . . . Jefferson was determined to make the United States an imperial contender." That this straightforward and comprehensible expansionist theme recurs in scholarly work suggests that its assertions are not implausible, not imperceptible, and not without merit.

Recent scholarship on the Doctrine of Discovery by Robert Miller, Eastern Shawnee, Lewis and Clark Law School professor, and member of the Bicentennial Circle of Tribal Advisors, illustrates the principles that underlie the impetus for the expedition. He dispels the popular belief that the Louisiana Purchase was a remarkable land deal because the United States did not buy the land in that transaction. If the United States had bought the land, the next century would not have been spent executing treaties with and buying land from tribes to acquire that territory. Instead, what the United States purchased were Napoleon's so-called discoverer's rights. Miller describes the chronological development and application of the Doctrine of Discovery, the philosophy and international law that crossed the Atlantic and took root in the fertile soil of the fledgling United States. "Discovery was applied by European/Americans to legally infringe on the real property and sovereign rights of the American Indian nations and their people, without their knowledge or consent, and it continues to adversely affect Indian tribes and people today. . . . The three fundamental tenets of American Indian law, the plenary power, the trust responsibility, and the tribal diminished sovereignty doctrines, which grant the United States nearly unchecked power in Indian affairs, all arose from the Doctrine of Discovery."

Miller demonstrates how the doctrine arises from Spain and Portugal when "the conversion of the 'nearly wild' infidel natives was justified because they allegedly did not have a common religion, were not governed by laws, lacked normal social intercourse, money, metal, writing, European style clothing, and lived like animals. . . ."

By 1493, the Church exercised the Doctrine of Discovery, explorers helped expand the Church's domain, Spain and Portugal had exclusive rights over other Christian countries to explore and colonize, and Spain and Portugal were sufficiently dominant to claim possession of lands simply through symbolic rituals.

Such routine institutionalized dehumanization of native peoples is not unique to Europe. The writings of Presidents George Washington and Thomas Jefferson provide ample evidence that they regarded the Indian inhabitants of North America as animals. In 1783, while a general, Washington recommended an approach for dealing with tribes summed up as "the Savage as Wolf," wherein rapidly encroaching civilization would eventually result in evacuation and attrition. Jefferson similarly suggested that for Indians who failed to assimilate "we shall be obliged to drive them with the beasts of the forests into the Stony mountains." If not dehumanization to help allay any threat Indians might represent, there was always the option of paternalism to diminish the power of the natives.

AUGUST 3RD, 1804   ... *The great chief of the Seventeen great nations of America, impelled by his parental regard for his newly adopted children on the troubled waters, has sent us to clear the road, remove every obstruction, and make it the road of peace between himself and his red children residing there.*

MERIWETHER LEWIS

The procedure for applying discoverer's rights through treaties was established and in use well before the expedition was dispatched. Between 1785 and 1789, when the United States entered into treaties with the Cherokee, Choctaw, Chickasaw, and Wyandot, the United States exerted "the sole and exclusive right of regulating the trade with the Indians and managing all their affairs in such manner as [the United States] think proper." In addition, in the four aforementioned treaties and the 1784 Treaty with the Six Nations (Iroquois) and the 1786 treaty with the Shawnee, the United States promised to protect the tribes and said they were "under the protection of the United States and of no other sovereign whatsoever." Professor Miller explains that the doctrine meant that "when European, Christian nations first discovered new lands the discovering country automatically gained sovereign and property rights in the lands of the non-Christian, non-European nation even though, obviously, the natives already owned, occupied, and used these lands."

The importance of Indians to President Jefferson is evidenced in many of his writings and speeches, including his second inaugural address and first, third, and sixth annual messages to the Senate and House of Representatives; in his work as a lawyer; as well as in his 1803 directives to Captain Lewis. Jefferson, a student of science, culture, and linguistics, author of the Declaration of Independence, was also a founding father of American archaeology, based on his excavation of Indian burial mounds. It can hardly be argued that he did not know what would become of the native peoples once the embrace of the United States reached them. In his second inaugural address on March 4, 1805, President Jefferson said:

> The aboriginal inhabitants of these countries I have regarded with the commiseration their history inspires. Endowed with the faculties and the rights of men, breathing ardent love of liberty and independence, and occupying a country which left them no desire but to be undisturbed, the stream of overflowing population from other regions directed itself on these shores; without power to divert, or habits to contend against, they have been overwhelmed by the current, or driven before it . . .

Miller demonstrates that "Jefferson clearly understood the ramifications of the Doctrine and utilized Discovery principles against the native people and tribal nations in the Louisiana and Pacific Northwest territories through the expedition." He also notes that the expedition was cited for more than three decades in political negotiations as justification for the United States' Discovery claim to the Pacific Northwest. The Doctrine of Discovery had been in use internationally for three centuries by 1803. By then, European and colonial governments, American state governments, and federal executive and legislative branches had adopted the doctrine.

So, was there a grand design in the acts of exploration carried out by Lewis and Clark? Unequivocally, yes. The expedition was in and of itself evidence of exercising the Doctrine of Discovery, affirmation of its efficacy, and manifestation of the expansionist dream. Miller summarizes: "Lewis and Clark carried out the tasks Jefferson assigned them in the Louisiana Territory to start to bring the tribes within the American political and commercial orbit and they performed well-recognized rituals in making the United States' Discovery claim to the Pacific Northwest . . . Lewis and Clark's actions seem to have been an amalgamation of all the Discovery rituals practiced by England, France, Spain, Holland, and Portugal, which included taking physical possession of land, building structures, official parades and formalistic procedures, native consent to European control, map-making, and astronomical observations."

Jefferson's recognition of tribes as sovereigns only made it more imperative that the expedition conduct ceremonial diplomacy councils, carve their names and dates on rocks and trees, brand what they could, erect improvements on the land, and name places and waterways and map them. Anyone who might attempt to preempt the U.S. interests would know that these Americans had already been there by the evidence they left. Peace medals in the form of U.S. currency and banners of the American interest in the form of the U.S. flag were doled out all along the routes traveled. The notice they posted at Fort Clatsop was a clear demarcation of the U.S. claim. This was an army expedition following the military orders of their commander in chief. Discovery was not just exploration. It was and is a legal construct complicating the standard historical narrative of the innocence of the expedition's journey.

So, if members of the expedition knowingly conducted reconnaissance with foresight and intent to dispossess Indians of their lands, should Americans still applaud their journey? Reluctantly, and conditionally, yes. When the United States and its citizens accept responsibility for the consequences that came after Lewis and Clark's mapping and recording, then they can praise a job done well. The members of the expedition were courageous, observant, astute, conscientious, and diligent about their duties. They were courageous because they were very far from home, vastly outnumbered by the Indians, and largely uneducated about the lands, conditions, and peoples in the West. Even when they were dangerously foolhardy in their methods or haphazard in conduct, they were still performing their duty. The various journals reflect these characteristics and permit a look into the changes that occurred during their contact with Indians as they transpired. These records of tribes in their homelands have been used in Indian land-claim cases because they represent documentation of our longitudinal occupancy and ownership. That the record they created might not win any journalistic laurels or spelling contests does not make their fieldwork and documentation any less worthwhile. That they were sometimes off the mark in cultural understanding or in measuring locations astronomically does not diminish the incredible record they created. That they were ignorant of the inherent knowledge and values in the ancient cultures they encountered does not separate them from many people today. That they were just following orders in preparing the homework for the dispossession of lands from American Indians does not distinguish them from more modern U.S. emissaries. They were a small military unit, representing a distant ambitious president leading an immature nation, doing the best they could with what they had at the time and within the mores with which they were born and raised. They were not "from the clouds" back then any more than they are idols to Indian peoples today.

AFTERMATH

. . . We require time to think, quietly, slowly.

PeoPeoMoxMox, Walla Walla
Treaty Council of 1855

The Louisiana Purchase and the Lewis and Clark expedition shaped the future boundaries of the young United States and changed our people's lives forever. Less than fifty years after Lewis and Clark trooped through the middle of the homelands of the Walla Walla, Umatilla, and Cayuse, our leaders ceded under duress—in peace-treaty proceedings—roughly 6 million acres of land to the United States. Washington territorial governor Isaac Stevens conducted a fourteen-month campaign to conclude ten treaties that would yield approximately 70 million acres of the Pacific Northwest to the United States by 1856. And he was not the only agent of empire at this time.

In the deliberations at the Walla Walla Treaty Council of 1855, Lewis and Clark are referenced many times. The minutes of the proceeding reflect that the treaty commissioners reminded those at the council that they "knew the Nes Perses were always friendly to the whites. Lewis and Clark had said this and all white men." Governor Stevens also asks, "What has made trouble between the white man and the red man? Did Lewis and Clark make trouble? They came from the Great Father; did I and mine make trouble? No! but the trouble had been made generally by bad white men and the Great Father knows it, hence laws." Then he extends the embrace of the United States typical in other treaties, "The Great Father therefore desires to make arrangements so you can be protected from these bad white men, and so they can be punished for their misdeeds."

Stevens again invokes Lewis and Clark to compliment and draw in the tribes: "The Great Father has learned much of you. He first learned of you from Lewis & Clarke, . . . they came through your country finding friends and meeting no enemies. I went back to the Great Father last year to say that you had been good, you had been kind, he must do something for you." In the same treaty council, Oregon superintendent of Indian Affairs Joel Palmer describes Discovery and Manifest Destiny. "It is but fifty years since the first white man came among you, those were Lewis and Clark who came down the Big River—the Columbia. Next came Mr. Hunt and his party, then came the Hudson's Bay Co. who were traders. Next came missionaries; these were followed by emigrants with wagons across the plains; and now we have a good many settlers in the country below you. . . . Like the grasshoppers on the plains; some years there will be more come than others, you cannot stop them; they say this land was not made for you alone. . . . Who can say that this is mine and that is yours? The white man will come to enjoy these blessings with you; what shall we do to protect you and preserve peace? There are but few whites here now, there will be many, let us like wise men, act so as to prevent trouble. . . . And now while there is room to select for you a home where there are no white men living let us do so. . . ."

The treaty commissioners repeatedly conveyed the urgency of their requirement to execute a treaty. By 1855, our people had spilled the blood of the missionaries Marcus and Narcissa Whitman among others, the Oregon Trail migration was twelve years old, the railroads needed to be transcontinental, gold had been discovered, and Spain and England had relinquished their claims in the Oregon Territory. After describing what he knows of Fort Laramie and California circumstances, the Nez Perce leader Eagle from the Light spoke about previous diplomatic gambits: "At the time the first white men ever passed through this country, although the people of this country were blind, it was their heart to be friendly to them. Although they did not know what the white people said to them they answered yes as if they were blind. . . . I have been talked to by the French and by the Americans, and one says to me, go this way, and the other says go another way; and that is the reason I am lost between them."

Through travel to other regions and through the talk of white men at the churches and trading posts, tribal leaders were aware of the colonialist enterprise at the time of the Treaty Council and well before. "Lawyer Said. This Earth is known as far as it extends. . . . We also know that towards the east there are a great many different kinds of people: there are red people and yellow people and black people, and a long time ago the people that travelled this country passed on the waters. . . . From this country they took back samples of rich earth, of flowers, and all such things; they also reported that there was a country on the other side, and it was peopled and these people reported they had found a country."*

Our spokesmen at the Treaty Council were not naïve, nor were they oblivious to the fact that decisions were being made for them without consultation or their consent. They were beset by the savage-as-wolf consequence, which was threatened in no uncertain terms. At the council, Cayuse leader Young Chief said, ". . . The reason why we could not understand you was that you selected this country for us to live in without our having any voice in the matter. . . . You embraced all my country, where was I to go, was I to be a wanderer like a wolf. Without a home without a house I would be compelled to steal, consequently I would die. I will show you lands I will give you, we will then take good care of each other. . . . I think the land where my forefathers are buried should be mine."

The tribal leaders were aware of what they were being asked to do and knew of the whites' perceptions of them as eager traders. Walla Walla leader PeoPeoMoxMox said, "In one day the Americans become as numerous as the grass; this I learned in California; I know that it is not right. You have spoken in a round about way; speak straight. I have ears to hear you and here is my heart. Suppose you show me goods shall I run up and take them? That is the way we are, we Indians, as you know us. Goods and the earth are not equal; goods are for using on the Earth. I do not know where they have given lands for goods."

*U.S. Department of the Interior, Bureau of Indian Affairs, *Certified Copy of the Original Minutes of the Official Proceedings at the Council in Walla Walla Valley, Which Culminated in the Stevens Treaty of 1855* (Portland, Ore.: Bureau of Indian Affairs, 1953).

Our tribal leaders were steadfast in their lack of desire to cooperate in the land cession. On one night, the Cayuse announced a lockdown in their camp, indicating no white visitors would be permitted. That night, they proposed to their tribal allies a war that would eliminate the whites and allow them to reclaim all their lands. But after their allies refused the proposition, they returned to hear the commissioners' proposals. After a week of council meetings, Governor Stevens made his plan clear. "I will now explain this matter more freely. We wish to put the Spokanes, the Nes Perces, the Walla Walla, the Cayuses, the Umatillas on one Reservation in the Nes Perces country." He would not prevail. He eventually agreed to create a third reservation, the one where most Cayuse, Walla Walla, and Umatilla live today.

Our leaders did not succumb to the tactics that had been so successfully applied in so many other councils. But our fate would be the one common to most Indians in the late nineteenth century. While some would become successful farmers and ranchers, most of our people would adjust to subsist on the fishing, hunting, gathering, trapping, and grazing rights reserved in our Treaty of 1855, without which our suffering would have been much worse. The government policies and practices in reservation life and boarding schools would further disenfranchise and fractionalize our people, but they would not do us in. We are still working to overcome the social, psychological, physical, and economic consequences of what followed Lewis and Clark. At great cost, our people have survived. In every major tribal decision-making point since, the troubles of our ancestors are revisited. We do not do this to remind ourselves of the injustices. We do so to remind ourselves of the wisdom, fortitude, forbearance, and foresight of our ancestors who made tremendous sacrifices so that we may still be here in our homeland and so that we follow their example.

The series of Isaac Stevens's treaties negotiated in 1854–56 provided the United States with the fulfillment of the dream of a continental nation reaching both coasts. President Jefferson and the

Founding Fathers charted the course; the Lewis and Clark expedition mapped and branded the route; and treaty commissioners imposed their national rights of Discovery on Indians who had few choices and none favorable. The unsettling of the West, the mess left by Manifest Destiny, is manifested in the lives of terminated tribes, unrecognized tribes, landless tribes, and tribes trying to restore the pedagogy of ancient cultures splintered by historical events and actors. Regardless of how many cultures live here now and who claims title to each parcel, this is the legacy of the young United States; it is the mutual inheritance of Americans.

In the Walla Walla Treaty Council of 1855, our leaders reserved for our tribes 512,000 acres so that we might continue to live according to the natural laws given to us by the Creator. Oregon was granted statehood February 14, 1859, prior to the official dispossession of our lands—almost a month before the treaty was ratified on March 8. The 512,000 acres became less than half that as a result of an eastern boundary dispute when the Umatilla Reservation was surveyed in 1871. It became 158,000 acres after the Slater Act of 1885 allotted lands to individual Indians and the U.S. government declared the balance to be surplus and open for settlement.

So, should enlightenment about past injustices and pursuit of justice be goals for future generations of non-Indian as well as Indian citizens, leaders, and officials? Absolutely, and progress should be assessed when planning anniversary observances. U.S. Constitution, article 6 states, "[A]ll Treaties made, or which shall be made, under the Authority of the United States, shall be the supreme Law of the Land." Ratified Treaty #289 is the treaty between the Cayuse, Umatilla, and Walla Walla Tribes and the United States. Our treaty rights face myriad challenges today, in the court of law and in the court of public opinion. There are citizens who believe that the treaties are not living documents, that they are out of date, obsolete, and no longer useful. Indeed, treaties were the means through which all others obtained legal title to Indian lands, and it would behoove non-Indians to protect and uphold the provisions of treaties today.

CONCLUSION

Our tribal history is as ancient as our bond to the place the Creator gave us in which to live. One of the recent modern chapters in our long history begins with the arrival of the army expedition led by Lewis and Clark into our homeland. American history in the interior Pacific Northwest commences with their arrival. Comparatively speaking, Americans are still the new kids on the block. American Indians were largely exempt from the American ideals of democracy, justice, domestic tranquillity, common defense, and general welfare for most of the past two centuries. The "Great White Father" could not provide what his voting citizenry did not require, and usually did not deliver on promises past presidents and congresses made to Indians. However, the land and cultural teachings sustained us.

This history was, is, and always will be a story about our land. The passage of time does not separate the story from the land, and our people have refused to be separated from this land. By now, it must be clear we are not going to go away or become extinct. The immense and powerful United States needs to acknowledge tribal contributions to its development. Our lands, knowledge, customs, sacred foods, and medicines have all been subjected to unwelcome harvests by unethical parties. And yet, tribes continue to try to inform and protect this still-young nation because this is our home. The United States is a powerful nation that must do what it has promised.

We have been patient. We are not leaving. But the land and the species that the Creator placed here with us need our help. The way we all live has consequences for water and air quality and affects all the other species with which we share this home. Our tribes have undertaken natural and cultural management compacts and plans and implemented a host of projects to restore and protect many parts of the ecosystem. There are many publicly owned lands in our homeland, and we are active participants in their future wherever possible. Also, with the revenue our tribal enterprises provide, we have begun buying back land, sometimes at seemingly rapacious rates, from the great-grandchildren of emigrant families. Our imperative is constant; our tribes must protect our home and all the gifts from the Creator.

My grandfather's great-grandfathers were little boys when the Lewis and Clark expedition came into our homeland. They would grow up and represent our people at the Walla Walla Treaty Council of 1855. In their lifetimes, the hospitality, sincerity, and honesty of their parents would not save them from the travesty and tragedy of the unsettling of the West. Their tribes went from being superior hosts to Lewis and Clark to being forced to cede almost all of their lands in their lifetimes.

"Our people's devotion to this land is stronger than any piece of paper," my grandfather told my mother, when explaining his World War I tour of duty in France with the U.S. Navy well before Indians had the right to vote. That's why he went to war when the United States had conflict with other countries. That devotion is deeper than our mistrust. It is more important than our wounds from past injustices. It is tougher than hatred. We continue to be inextricable from our homeland. However modern our tools and wars become, our bond to the place the Creator gave us is immovable since time immemorial.

PART TWO

Mandan and Hidatsa
of the Upper Missouri

Gerard A. Baker

GERARD A. BAKER, Mandan-Hidatsa, is a member of the tribe on whose lands the Lewis and Clark expedition wintered in 1804–1805. Baker has spent most of his twenty-seven years in government service in the midwestern/northwestern region through which the expedition traveled. He has held a variety of posts within both the National Park Service and the USDA Forest Service, three of them of considerable significance, symbolically, in the context of U.S. history. First, he was superintendent of the Little Bighorn Battlefield National Monument, where his work earned him an NPS Intermountain Regional Director's Award. In September 2000, he was named superintendent of the Lewis and Clark National Historic Trail. For the next four years he was responsible for the trail's management and the traveling exhibit "Corps of Discovery II: 200 Years to the Future," working with fifty-eight Indian tribes and nineteen trail states. Finally, in May 2004, he took over as superintendent of the world-famous Mount Rushmore National Memorial, the huge, carven images representing four U.S. presidents and 150 years of American history. Amidst all the above, Gerard Baker has had time for a family (wife, Mary Kay, and four children) and several Indian-related hobbies—historical research, oral history of the northern plains, and traditional crafts such as brain tanning.

MANDAN AND HIDATSA
OF THE UPPER MISSOURI

The Corps of Discovery . . . One of Many

When I think back to my early days on our ranch about nine miles northwest of Mandaree, North Dakota, I remember the visits of many of the elders from the Fort Berthold Indian Reservation from both sides of my family, Mandan and Hidatsa. My mother's side were descendants of the Hidatsa villages and matrilineal, whereas my father's side were descendents of the Mandan villages. I heard many stories of our people and the villages when we lived on the mouth of the Knife River and the Big Missouri River near what is today the small village of Stanton, North Dakota. In remembering the stories I heard and the many people who visited our villages, I remember not hearing much about the famed trip of Lewis and Clark. As some would say later, they were no big deal to our people, as our tribes had dealt with white trappers and traders for many, many years, and I was told that "we were used to the speeches." What was remembered and told to me was the story of the first black man our people ever saw and of course the young woman who was married to the French trapper, Charbonneaux. The black man was of course the slave York, and the young woman we Hidatsa know as Sakakawea. There are many stories about this Sakakawea and who she was. I will tell one that I remember. I remember hearing this in different parts from several different people, but I remember this version from my father, the late Paige Baker, Sr.

He told me that our people, now called the Mandan and Hidatsa (he was almost a full-blood Mandan, and Mandan was his first language), were known to have lived in five villages on the Knife and Missouri rivers. Our creation stories tell us that we had three subtribes of Hidatsas and two subtribes of Mandan. From north to south, the villages were the homes of the Hidatsa, Awatxia, and Awaxixa (now these groups are all called under the general name of Hidatsa). The Mandan, he said, had lived in two villages. He said there were more villages in the old, old days, but he always heard only of the two where he said the bands called the Nuptadi and the Nuitadi (the languages spoken by these were later classified as dialects) had lived, and it was the people of these villages who had pretty much kept the Corps of Discovery alive, given them information regarding the tribes upstream, and shown them the "lay of the land." Each of these tribes had their own creation stories, and each would live in different areas in and around the Missouri River and not just in the village locations that are outlined today.

It was one of these peoples, the Awaxia, he said, where Sakakawea came from. When she was born, her group had been away from the Missouri River, which was common in that time, and had lived in a fortified village that was located on a high bluff but several miles up the Little Missouri River, in the Badlands of what is now North Dakota. The leader of the village went by the name of Twilight Walker or Nightwalker. My father said he had this name due to the fact that he would use the evening time to pray, as that "time" was his medicine. The area today is called Nightwalker's Butte, and one can still find remains of the village, including the cottonwood posts that were part of the lodges and the palisades. What made this village unique is that it was built on a very steep plateau with only one way to enter, so it had a natural fortification, as well as a built fortification made from cottonwood trees and a ditch that was dug around the village. The dirt from this ditch was used for the earth-lodge construction, so it served several purposes, including providing a defense around the village. It was here that my father and other elders say Sakakawea was born. I never heard a date, as the people never had actual dates, but seasons, and they never mentioned what season Sakakawea was born in. I never heard who her parents were, but they did say that she was one of several children. She grew up in the Awatxia world of clans and societies, being taught by her elder clan relatives. The clan system is matrilineal, meaning your mother's side had many responsibilities as the teachers. The societies are age-grade organizations, and you would change societies as you got older, many times following your family's line of societies. The people of this village, like many others, would have lived an agriculture-based life, but in those early days, they had subsisted on hunting and gathering as well. It was the responsibility of the men to hunt and protect the village and, as was the custom, when the men went out hunting they would usually leave behind some younger boys to defend the people, and of course the old men would always stay, so they too would protect the village. It was at these times that the village was the most vulnerable to the tribes that were considered enemies. One of these tribes was the Shoshone, whose name means "from the west."

As my father's version of the story goes, the Hidatsa men were all out hunting when the Shoshone attacked the village, not only killing the defenders left behind, but also taking some of the children and women, Sakakawea and her brother being among those taken. They

View of the Mandan Village *by George Catlin.*
Courtesy of the National Gallery of Art.

were taken back to Shoshone territory in the mountains, and the young ones were then raised as Shoshone. It was told that Sakakawea was old enough to remember where she came from, and, as time went on, she would look to the east, toward the way she had come, and remember her village and cry for her family. She was noticed by an old woman of the Shoshone, and that old lady, it is said, took pity on her. One day she told Sakakawea that she knew she missed her people and that she would help her get home. She told her to prepare for her journey and that, as the sun set the next day, she should go once again and look toward the east, but this time she would see a wolf, as this was the old lady's helper, and the young girl was to follow that wolf each night; when morning came, the wolf would go away, and it was at that time that Sakakawea should hide. She told her that four wolves would lead her back to her people. Sakakawea then went to her brother and told him what this old lady had said. He replied that if it was true that they came from the villages to the east, he did not remember, as he was very young when they brought him to this village, and because of that, he considered this to be his village and his people, and that someday he would be a leader among them. She did not argue, but said her good-bye and got her things ready for the next night when she would sneak out of the village. The next evening, she sneaked away from the village and as she stood looking to the east, just as the old lady had said, a wolf appeared. The wolf would trot ahead, then look back; on the fourth time it did this, she followed. As the old lady said, each wolf would stay just far enough ahead so Sakakawea could follow; she did this for four nights. Now, as I mentioned, the people at that time had no concept of "time" in the modern sense, so the "four" could be translated to mean four days, or four weeks. The number four also represents the four sacred directions of the Earth. It was told to me that Sakakawea not only lived off the fruits and berries of the land, meaning her journey took place in the time when the berries were ripe, early summer perhaps. Each wolf also killed game for her and would leave it on the trail so that she could cook and eat meat as well. This is the way that Sakakawea made it back to the village of her people, the Hidatsa, according to my father, who heard this story as a young man himself.

When I was very young we used to have a blind uncle live with us on occasion; his name was Thad Mason. He was a man that was a great singer and could remember many old songs and told stories of this. The tribal historian, Mr. Calvin Grinnell from the Fort Berthold Indian Reservation, offered the following articles regarding the Sakakawea story. Had I been older, I could have had the opportunity to ask my uncle Thad many questions. . . .

VAN HOOK REPORTER
APRIL 2, 1925

BULLSEYE'S STORY OF SAKAKAWEA
TO MAJOR WELCH IN COUNCIL

My name is Bullseye. I am of the Hidatsa (Gros Ventre). I have seen 58 winters. I was a scout at the mouth of the Yellowstone River. I was at Fort Abraham Lincoln, too, when I was young. My father's name was Lean Bull. He was Hidatsa; he was a brave man. My mother's name was Otter Woman. She was Hidatsa. I was four years old when she was killed by an enemy. She died sitting up against a wagon wheel. My grandmother died of a wound in her side.

The name of my mother's mother was Sakakawea. She was my grandmother. The father of my grandmother was Smoked Lodge. He was Hidatsa. He signed the treaty of 1825. The mother of my grandmother was Otter Woman. She was Hidatsa, too. My grandmother Sakakawea had a brother whose name was Cherry Necklace. He lived with our relatives, the Crows, in Montana. They are sometimes called the Absarokas, but they are Hidatsa. They went away from us a long time ago. My grandmother had a half brother whose name was One Buffalo.

When my grandmother was 18 years old, her father gave her to a white man. She married this white man, who was my grandfather. His name was Sharbonish. He lived among the Mandans and Hidatsas then. That was at the village of the Knife River. This white man and Sakakawea had several children; the first one was a man child. The second was a woman child. They named her Otter Woman. She was my mother (the birth sign was given by Bullseye here). The third child was a woman child, too, the fourth child was a woman child. They named them Cedar Woman and Different Breast. The father of all these children was Sharbonish. You have called it a little different, but it is the same man. None of these descendants are alive now except myself. They are all dead from the enemy or the sickness.

The same year when my grandfather took Sakakawea away from the lodge (her father's lodge) they went far away somewhere. They went toward the west and were gone for a long time and traveled far. They went so far they were among people who sometimes went to the ocean out beyond there. This was on the other side of the mountains beyond the three rivers of the Missouri. They went past these three rivers. Then they went on over to another river which flowed the other way. All the rivers there flowed that way. When they came to a very bad river (Salmon River) they turned back. They came back to the Knife River then.

So she knew that country. This was the year before that white party came among us. They (Lewis and Clark) stayed there (Fort Mandan) that winter. When these people came (1804) they selected Sharbonish and Sakakawea to guide them into that same country where she had been the year before, because Sakakawea and Sharbonish knew that country then.

We have heard that they wrote that she was not a Hidatsa. They say she was a Shoshoni among us. She was not a Shoshoni. Everybody knew them. They knew her father and mother, too. The interpreter got it wrong and it has been wrong ever since then, so they wrote it wrong. It is hard to interpret right. When the interpreter gets tired or is not very good in both languages, he sometimes talks the easiest way. These white men were told that my grandmother knew that country

Interior of Mandan Earth Lodge. *Illustration by George Catlin.*

well. She had been there and had traveled across the mountains. The interpreter told them she had a brother there. That is Indian relationship. It did not mean that the Gros Ventres (Hidatsa) had taken her captive from the Shoshoni. Perhaps her father, Smoked Lodge, had taken her up there on that trip, too. So the interpreter and the white man thought they had captured her and brought her back to live with the Hidatsa. We are sorry that they got it wrong. It has been wrong ever since.

They (Lewis and Clark) started in boats and pulled the boats in some places. Where the banks were good they used a small mule which the whites had on the boat to pull along the shore. Then they would put the mule back on the boat. They went to those three rivers and there over the mountains to the ocean. While there my grandmother got many good shell ornaments from that place.

When they came back (1806) they were on a large raft in the Yellowstone River. They passed through the country of our relatives, the Crows. They passed a large camp of those jealous people (the Crow Indians) at Sitting Bear Bill's place. Sakakawea called out to the people and asked if her brother was in the camp. She said for him to go on down the river beyond the next bend and she would have the white boat land there. They landed just as she said and her brother was there. His name was Cherry Necklace, and he wanted to make her a good present there. He had a very fine white horse; trained buffalo horse. This is a very good present and he gave his white horse to Sharbonish. They loaded it on the boat and brought it to our village. Sakakawea gave him some fine shell ornaments to wear. The Crows had good horses.

I will tell you how my grandmother Sakakawea died. My mother, Otter Woman, died at the same time nearly. This place was in Montana. It was near where Glasgow is now. It was on a creek. I think they called it Sand Creek. When my grandmother, Sakakawea, was married to this man Sharbonish, she had learned to like coffee terribly well. She could not get along without coffee. When she got out of coffee she would travel a long distance to get some more. She saved the coffee from the pots and would put it on her head so it would smell like coffee.

During one of these trips to a trader's place to get coffee she was with two wagons with oxen hitched to them. My grandmother and my own mother, Otter Woman, and myself were in the party. I was only four years old so [I] do not remember who the rest were. We were on this creek near Glasgow one time and camped there. There was a trader's place not many miles away and we were going there to trade.

I was asleep on the ground between the hind wheels of the wagon by the side of my grandmother; my mother was under the front wheels. During the night I was awakened by shooting; the camp was attacked by some enemy; the men were firing through the wheels.

My mother said to [my] grandmother, "Take the child to the willow gulch." So Sakakawea took me by the arm and we ran into the brush of the gully there. The firing of the guns kept on for a while and then quit. All the yelling had ceased. My grandmother took me out then and we went back to the wagon. It was early in the morning when we left that coulee (their shelter). I can remember it well. I have never forgotten it.

Several people lay there dead around and under the wagons. My mother was sitting up against a wheel of one of the wagons. She had been struck and was badly wounded there.

My grandmother was also hit in the side with a bullet, but did not say anything about that. My grandmother did not cry any. My mother said, "Take the boy to the trader's place. I am dying now. The boy is yours to look after now."

She died there against the wheel then. That was the last I heard her say. But she pointed to her mother's (Sakakawea's) side and signed for her to go away. So we walked over the hills and prairies to the trader's store. Sakakawea, my grandmother, died at the trader's place from her wound several days after that time.

This, Major Welch believes, is the true story of the death of Sakakawea, the "bird woman" of the Mandan and Gros Ventres villages, who guided Lewis and Clark. It is but one of the tragic stories known to all the Indians of those tribes.

The old woman of Stourer; the "wife of Charbonneau" of Luttig; the Sacajawea of Dr. Hebard—these stories may not be substantiated, but this story of Bulls Eye rings true. Dr. Eastman may discover among the men of the Yanktonais or Assiniboine someone who was a member of the war party who killed Sakakawea. If her grave should not be found, I would say that the proper place for the monument is somewhere in the vicinity of the present Fort Clark in North Dakota, where she lived practically all her life long.

Major Welch cites the names of the following Indians as present when Bulls Eye told his story: Birds Bill, Chief of the Old Scout Society; Dog, called George Parshall; Stanley Bean, an educated Indian; Henry Bad Gun, a descendant of Four Bears, former Gros Ventre (Hidatsa) chief, noted in the Lewis and Clark memoirs; Black Chest, an old U.S. volunteer scout; Looking and Hunts Along, called Thad Mason; Arthur Mandan, son of Chief Bad Cow who was the son of Scared Face. The latter was Welch's interpreter.

"Sakakawea was born in 1787 and was 17 years old when employed by Lewis and Clark in 1804–5; Bulls Eye, her grandson, was four years old when she was killed in the fight at the wagon train; Bulls Eye was born in 1865 for his age is now 60 (?); consequently the Bird Woman was killed when she was 82 years old in 1869," is the final summary of Major Welch.

Also, another interesting bit of information . . .

A significant and intriguing point supporting Bulls Eye's story of Sakakawea's tribal origin, the obituary of the baby who made the perilous journey, was written by an editor who knew Jean Baptiste Charbonneau for fourteen years prior to his death. It should be noted that the Crow were originally a band of the Hidatsa just a few centuries ago and we retain many familial ties to this day.

Death of a California Pioneer—We are informed by . . . a letter announcing the death of J. B. Charbonneau, who left this country some weeks ago, with two companions, for Montana Territory. The letter is from one of the party, who says Mr. C., was taken sick with mountain fever, on the Owyhee, and died after a short illness.

Mr. Charbonneau was known to most of the pioneer citizens of this region of country, being himself one of the first adventurers (into the territory now known as Placer county) upon the discovery of gold; where he has remained with little intermission until his recent departure for the new gold field, Montana, which, strangely enough, was the *land of his birth* [emphasis mine], whither he was returning in the evening of life, to spend the few remaining days that he felt was in store for him.

Mr. Charbonneau was born in the western wilds, and grew up a hunter, trapper, and pioneer, among that class of men of which Bridger, Beckwourth, and other noted trappers of the woods were the representatives. He was born in the country of the Crow Indians—his father being a Canadian Frenchman, and his mother *a half breed of the Crow tribe* [emphasis mine]. He had, however, better opportunities than most of the rough spirits, who followed the calling of trapper, as when a young man he went to Europe and spent several years, where he learned to speak, as well as write several languages. At the breaking out of the Mexican War he was on the frontiers, and upon the organization of the Mormon Battalion he was engaged as a guide and came with them to California.

Subsequently upon the discovery of gold, he, in company with Jim Beckwourth, came upon the North Fork of the American river, and for a time it is said were mining partners. . . . The reported discoveries of gold in Montana, and the rapid peopling of the Territory, excited the imagination of the old trapper, and he determined to return to the scenes of his youth. . . .

There are many stories and many claims as to who Sakakawea was. I personally believe that we will never know, but what is important to understand is that, whoever she was and whichever tribe she belonged to, she was very well respected by Lewis and Clark and she did play a very important role in the voyage to the West and back. Some things to consider as we discuss this famed lady and who her "family" and tribe really were—Hidatsa or Shoshone: If she really was born and raised among the Shoshone, why did she not run away from her husband, as he was supposed to be very mean and would beat her? Why did she not stay with her people, the Shoshone, and why did she come back to the Hidatsa village? Or did she know that the Hidatsa were the people she was born into? Another thought, regarding her brother—we all know the story of how excited she got when she realized that she was meeting him, as in the story I heard told. Was he too a Hidatsa, but preferred to stay behind, or could he have been an "adopted" brother from her trip out West? I can remember the elders, including my father, talking about this and, of course, we say, she is one of us.

Like all the tribes that encountered the "famed" Lewis and Clark, we have had a history of struggle and survival over the last two hundred years that included forced religions, boarding schools, relocation etc., etc., but we are still here and we continue to move ahead. As the elders said, Lewis and Clark were no big deal, but we knew how to be diplomats from earlier encounters, and we knew the value of trade, and I think we understood that the expedition was just the continuation of many *maashe's* (white men) to come.

At the time of Lewis and Clark we had already suffered our first smallpox epidemic, but even with that, we were still a strong people and dominated the river trade. What Lewis and Clark didn't see, or at least maybe chose not to write about, or as some elders speculated, they did not understand, was the interaction among families, and the responsibilities of the members of the various clans and societies.

Each family and tribe has their stories, and if nothing else, I pray that the Lewis and Clark story will be only a stepping-stone to continue to bring out the truths of the Indian people and the story of our struggle and survival.

We will never go away.

WE YA OO YET SOYAPO

Allen V. Pinkham, Sr.

ALLEN V. PINKHAM, SR., is a highly respected executive of the Nez Perce, the Indian tribe that, more than any other, had established favorable connections with Meriwether Lewis, William Clark, Sacagawea, York, and other members of the Corps of Discovery. In 1981 Pinkham was elected to the Nez Perce Tribal Executive Committee (NPTEC), the governing body of the Nez Perce Tribe, on which he served two years as vice chairman and five years as chairman. He also served as president of the Affiliated Tribes of Northwest Indians (ATNI) for two years and as vice president of the National Congress of American Indians (NCAI) for two years. He has spent much of his adult life as a representative of the Nez Perce nation in the Northwest and throughout the United States, culminating in recent positions relating to the Lewis and Clark Bicentennial Commemoration. He was re-elected to the National Museum of the American Indian (MNAI) Board of Trustees under the Smithsonian Institution.

Before his emergence in leadership roles, Pinkham had been variously a U.S. Marine corporal, a forest-fire fighter, a lab technician, a logger, and a production supervisor for the manufacture and packaging of bullets and pistol ammunition. He also served as a tribal liaison with the USDA Forest Service.

Call him an oral historian or a storyteller, Allen Pinkham is a skillful presenter of his people's culture and traditions. He lectures widely and is co-author with Dan Landeen of *Salmon and His People*, published in 1999 by Confluence Press.

WE YA OO YET SOYAPO

*T*he following stories are the oral history and culture of the Ni Mii Puu (ne-mee-poo; Nez Perce People), as we foresaw a great changing time two and three hundred years ago. The stories include the history of the author's family and where they lived at Ciwikite (downriver from Spalding, Idaho). The author's ancestors greeted the Corps of Discovery in 1805 and 1806.

A new animal came into our country approximately the year 1700. As we viewed this animal many questions would have been asked: What use is this animal? What does it eat? How do you care for it? Is it like the dog? And most important, where does it come from? Oh! It comes to this Island (America) from across the eastern bitter water (Atlantic Ocean). This animal we called sikem (sik-em; horse).

Because of the horse many new adventures and discoveries occurred, and we found a new kind of human being. Prior to Lewis and Clark these human beings lived east of us for three hundred years, so how could we not know about these people? This new creature, once we decided it was human, we called Soyapo (so-ya-poo; Across Water People, aka White People).

The Soyapo brought good and bad things to us. Most were tragic. Yet today we are still here in our own country within the United States, making the best of the situation. We are active in the social and economic structure as we were for the last five hundred years. Love of country and knowing Hunyawat (huny-a-waat; the Creator) watches over us has sustained the Nez Perce people. Here we shall remain until the One Who Made This Earth takes it away.

The following stories contain Nez Perce words spelled first by the linguistic standard, followed in parentheses by a hyphenated phonetic spelling and the English meaning. This method gives readers the flavor of the Nez Perce language. At other times, terms or names are translated into English and used in the text as such. The phonetic spelling appears only at first mention.

According to Harry Wheeler, a noted Nez Perce tribal historian and storyteller (ca. 1890s–1963), the Nez Perce word we ya oo yit *means "the coming." Soyapo is the name the Nez Perce adopted for white people, but its origin is a description of those who came across the Atlantic Ocean to our Island—the Americas.*

PROLOGUE

The Ni Mii Puu (ne-mee-poo; the Real People, or Nez Perce People) have occupied the upper reaches of the Columbia Basin along the Snake, Clearwater, and Salmon rivers since time immemorial and were created by Ice ye ye (itsi-yea-yea; Coyote) along the banks of the Clearwater River. In present-day north-central Idaho, southeastern Washington, and northeastern Oregon, we had a good life! We could collect all that was provided by our Creator: salmon (five species of the anadromous fish), deer, moose, elk, and buffalo, *qimes* and cous roots, berries, and medicines to help cure ourselves when we became ill. But those elders who knew or foretold what would happen to the Ni Mii Puu said a great change was coming and the earth would be turned over and the rivers would run red with our blood. And they said every third generation* something good or bad would happen to the Nii Mii Puu and it would take five generations for the people to recover from this great change.

One day, a pale-faced *hanit* (hawn-it; creature) would be coming behind a white-faced animal about the size of a deer and would come through Lapwai (lap-way) Valley. Was this pale-faced creature a human being? Maybe it was half human because it didn't look like us? It spoke a language we had never heard before; it had body odor and had eyes like fish. Some of them would have their faces on upside down! Would this creature have a heart? We would find that this new kind of human being had an ability we did not have. It

---

*Three generations is approximately one hundred years.

could make marks on *times* (tee-mus; paper), and a different person could read word for word what those marks meant. They could make things we could not. Glass and metal were new to us. They were inventive and aggressive, but sometimes their minds didn't work right and they killed for no reason. There would be great misunderstandings and culture conflicts. They would push around and abuse our elders. They would draw lines across the earth, and they would say, "This is mine, and this is yours." They would point to things and say, "This is mine, and this is mine, and this is mine!" We would undergo a great change if we were to survive. They would have a different way with the Creator and how they lived with the bounty of the earth. There would be many thousands upon thousands of these new kinds of people where the sun came up!

In 1903 a small Ni Mii Puu boy, who would become known as Qelxel Qine (khul-khul qew-neh; Old Man Spider), whose English name became Alexius Michael Pinkham, would listen to three old men tell of this great change as they saw it occur and how the people understood that it would happen.

LAND DESCRIPTION

In north-central Idaho, on the Clearwater River near the mouth of Lapwai Creek, on both sides of the river, flat areas have been long occupied by Ni Mii Puu. Two hundred years ago, this area had a large population and became the first occupation site of non-Indians— first the mission site and later the Indian-agency building that "enforced" the new reservation system. Today, it is still near the center of tribal operations at Lapwai, Idaho. In the winter of 1903, long tents* were set up, and the Nez Perce people gathered on these flats just as they had since time immemorial. They would reminisce and tell of events that changed the lifeways of the people. The year 1903

*A long tent is an A-frame structure utilizing canvas and poles.

marked the beginning of the Lewis and Clark Centennial, and the memory of the contact was still fresh in the minds of many tribal elders, descendants of those who greeted the explorers. Many of the stories told by the elders were of the strangers who came to our land, lost, hungry, and tired, but many of the stories told of a time before the human beings came upon the earth. By 1903, instead of the village with its bustle of Indian life, the area had become restricted by the Dawes Act,* which was applied on the Nez Perce Indian Reservation in 1893 by Alice Fletcher and company (i.e., the Bureau of Indian Affairs). The immediate area of the long tents, and later a longhouse of sawed planks built in about 1920, became reduced because of non-Indians' subsequent settlement onto historic, tribally owned land. A railroad and railroad bridge, constructed in 1899, bisected the flats as well. Eventually a National Park Service site and museum would occupy most of the area above and below the mouth of Lapwai Creek.

The area described is highly regarded by Nez Perce people because many good memories still exist about this land. In the 1920s, a *kuhet iiniit* (koo-het-eneet; wood-plank longhouse) was built a short distance below the railroad bridge on the south side of the Clearwater River but was destroyed by a flood in 1964. Immediately above the railroad bridge is a place called in English "the boom grounds," although it is known to the Nez Perce as the "Taking Out Place," because there they could get lumber and firewood that drifted down the river at flood time and piled on the banks. The Nez Perce also snagged wood and logs out of the currents with hooks thrown out and pulled in with long ropes. The practice was killed when Dworshak Dam was constructed on the north fork of the Clearwater in the 1970s. Many of these happenings were foretold by our Ni Mii Puu ancestors.

At a place on the south bank and 360 steps above the mouth of Lapwai Creek is Ice ye ye Tekash (itsi-yea-yea tee-kash; Coyote's Cra-

---

*The Dawes Act broke up the reservation into allotments of 160 acres or less for each Indian.

dle Board). It is set upright in the ground and is a flat local stone eight feet high. In 1923 the Daughters of the American Revolution (DAR) had found this stone lying near the hill, erected it, and secured a placard to it to memorialize Reverend Henry Spalding. Reverend Spalding, in 1836, had built a log cabin for his family a few steps away from the 1923 erected stone. The stone is now on National Park Service ground, and, three hundred steps farther upstream, the longhouse site is on Nez Perce tribal ground. The long-tent site of 1903 is between the Coyote's Cradle Board monument and the wood-plank longhouse.

At the long-tent site an eight-year-old Ni Mii Puu *hacwal* (ne-mee-poo hahs-wal; Nez Perce boy) would learn many things about his people. In 1903 three elderly Nez Perce men would gather at one of the long tents and talk; the boy would listen. Their names were Pakaowna (pa-ka-ow-na), Panickonee, and Neshne Qine (nesh-nah qew-neh; Old Man Cut Nose). The meanings of the first and second names are lost to antiquity. The owner of the third name, "Cut Nose," aka John Cutnose, was the boy's uncle, age sixty, who was

This stone is Coyote's first son's cradle board and also serves as Reverend Spalding's monument. This National Park Service photo depicts the stone as it was erected by the DAR in 1923.

*This photo was taken a few yards from where the previous
photo was taken. Note the hills in the horizon. This* kuhetiniit
*[koo-het-eneet], or longhouse, was called a long tent after
canvas was acquired. This is where the three elderly men
would attend the traditional Indian ceremonial gatherings.*

the grandson of the Cut Nose mentioned in the Lewis and Clark
journals. The first Cut Nose and other leaders contributed mightily
to the expedition by guiding and by map-drawing the area, from the
land of the Chinooks in the west to the land of Blackfeet in the
east, showing the lands they were very familiar with. He spoke of
how the Nez Perce traveled the country. He also helped guide the
Corps of Discovery along the rivers and across the Camas Prairie to
Kamiah.

TIME AND TRAVEL

When the Nez Perce traveled they spoke of how many days it took to
reach a landmark or referenced the phases of the moon for longer

travel. Seasons, or when certain plants bloomed or other resources became available for use, are referenced also. Travel is marked by days or before and after midday to reach a point. Then short distance was measured by steps. Travel could be by foot, by horse, or upstream or downstream by canoe. The important element was the time it took to travel, not the actual distance, because timing was essential to meeting people at a landmark. Also signs could be left at known landmarks to let others know you had passed by first and they were behind you—for example, the post-office cairns on the *kuseyniskit* (ku-se-in-is-kit; buffalo trail), or what is presently called the Lewis and Clark Trail, through the Bitterroot Mountains of Idaho.

CUT NOSE

The three elderly men would start by asking each other, "What do you want to know about? The future, present, or a long time ago?" On one occasion, John Cutnose said, "Let's talk of a time long ago when my grandfather received his name." "*Ehe* [ii heh; yes]," agreed the other two men. Cut Nose continued: "My grandfather was strong and a fighting *miyoxat* [mee-oo-khut; leader], who protected his people at a village called Yaxtoin [yakh-too in; Ridge Between Two Streams]. It's also known as the 'Salmon Jumping Over Place.' The Yaxtoin village is three miles upriver from here, but on the north side at the mouth of Potlatch River, although at that time Lewis and Clark called it after one of their men named Colter. My *tota* [grandfather] said these strange men and one Mountain Sheepeater [Lemhi] woman with a child came and asked questions about how people lived and how many lived here. Her name was Sacajawea and she was *hamolic* [ha-mo-lets; cute]; she was well liked by nearly everyone. Through many languages and hand-sign talk they asked about the rivers and mountains, so Tota drew a map for them, from the lands of the Chinooks to the lands of the Blackfeet. For this, Cut Nose, my grandfather, received a *kicuy* [coin] that says 'peace and friendship' on it. He kept this coin all his life, and when he went to the other side, we buried the peace medal with him. My grandfather was buried at Yaxtoin, and when this railroad was built, the railroad workers exposed and destroyed his grave and took the peace medal. We don't know why the Soyapo wanted to have this medal and destroyed graves! This medal was gone, and we don't know where it is, maybe back east. Sometimes their minds don't work right!

"One man with them [the expedition members] seemed to know hand-sign talk *tac* [tots; good]; he was of the eastern tribal Tito'oqan [teh-toh-qan; American Indians] whom we called 'With Sores People' because they had suffered smallpox before we had. He was a mixed-blood. His name was George Drewyer; he understood the ways of the Tito'oqan, was treated well, given gifts and a good horse. Lewis and Clark asked how my grandfather got his name." Cut Nose then began reminiscing. "This is the story of my grandfather's naming. . . .

"Cut Nose and a few other fighting men went south, to the country of the Tewelka [te-wel-ka; Enemy to Be Fought], also known as the Shoshone-Bannock people, seeking retribution for killing of some Nez Perce people, which had occurred earlier. We cannot remember why the killing started because the first killing happened so long ago. The fighting group met the Tewelka on the trail and challenged them to have a war. As they engaged in warfare, Cut Nose and a Tewelka fought with lances around a large chest-high stone. Cut Nose suffered a lance cut across his nose but he soon felled his foe and the Ni Mii Puu came away victorious. Before the fighting group returned to Yaxtoin, a messenger was sent ahead to tell the people to gather so that the story could be told and mourning could be done for those lost. My grandfather rode his horse around the village with the others of the fighting group, sang a victory song, and each told of the great adventure and what they did in the fighting. From that day forward my grandfather would be known as Neshne Qine [nee-shnee qewneh; Cut Nose, Older in Later Years]. A name well earned and known to all Ni Mii Puu!

"*Waco qalo!* [wah-koh ka-loh; That's all!]"

TRAVELERS

One of the old men said, "A good naming for your grandfather, but let's tell of a time long before we had seen Lewis and Clark. How did we know these strange people were coming to our country? Well, we knew many of these people were east of the great river that flowed east from the Bitterroot Mountains and then flowed south to the salt water. We knew this island (America) was surrounded by salt water. How did we know? Because we went to many places to find out about these people. We went north to a great lake. We went east to five great lakes where red pipe stone was found for our smoking pipes. And we heard of the strange people, then went to a place called Cincinnati where we found them. We went west past a mountain called by coast Indians 'Tahoma' [Mount Rainier]. We went south to a country that was hot all year long, and there we found a little animal that we called *pits quy yet* [piits-khoo-ee-yet; imitator]. It's now called the monkey. In this south country we saw another kind of people that wore hats and little blankets They called themselves Spanish and were Across Water People also."

The young boy asks a question: "How did we know how to travel across this island? I would get lost in those big prairies, and those mountains are so big and high!"

"Listen to this, Little Spider Boy. We will tell of a time when only animals were on this earth and no human beings. All the animals could talk among themselves and understand each other well. All birds, insects, fish, and animals could talk with each other, and this period was called 'Legends Times.' It was when the human beings came that all animals became mute. They complained because we used them for food, so they said, 'If you use us for food we will not talk to you anymore. We were on this earth first, and now you have to make an agreement with us on how to live on this earth.' After a great council, it was agreed that all animal species would be mute and it would be difficult for the human beings to catch and use them all. In exchange, the human beings would be separate from the animals but would watch over them because they could not speak for themselves among the human beings. This was the agreement we had with all living things on this earth. Offerings would be made for the sacrifice of life they would give for our benefit."

LEGENDS TIMES

The time before human beings, Old Wolf was sitting down and looking up at the sky. Along came Coyote, and he asked Old Wolf "What are you looking at?"

"*Unah!* [un-ah; Oh!] I'm looking at two of them—don't you see them?—grizzly bears!"

Coyote sat and looked up and saw them. In the meantime, Old Wolf's four younger brothers came along and asked the same question: "What are you looking at?"

Old Wolf replied, "We are looking at two grizzly bears. I sure wish I could go up there and look at them." Old Wolf was persistent and kept saying, "I sure wish I could go up there and look at them." Finally, Coyote said, "I will show you how to get up there." Coyote made a bow and five bundles of arrows. He shoots the first arrow into the sky, and it stays up there. He shoots the second arrow, and it sticks to the first arrow. The third arrow sticks to the second, and so forth, until the arrow path comes all the way to the ground.

Coyote said, "Now you can go up there and look at the grizzly bears." Old Wolf's next-oldest brother said, "I want to go up first with my next-oldest brothers and look at the grizzly bears." Old Wolf agreed. So the three wolf brothers went up the arrow way, sat, and looked across at the two bears. Old Wolf said, "I want to go up next with my youngest brother, and I will take my little dog with me." So they went up the arrow way, sat, and looked across at the two grizzly bears! They remain in the sky to this day!

Coyote stated, "When the human beings come, they will look up and see two grizzly bears, five wolf brothers, and one little dog!" That's all!

The teaching with this story is that the two grizzly bears line up with the North Star, and they rotate around the North Star and have a different position throughout the year. When youngsters hear this story the North Star is always in the same place for north. East and west are easy to find with the rising and setting of the sun. Now the four directions are known, and distant travel can be done.

A sun pole is another indicator of seasonal change and sun's position for the winter and summer solstice. A pole would be set upright near the village and the tip of the pole's shadow would be marked to show when it was shortest or longest for the year. Also the shadows of mountains would be used in the same way.

COYOTE'S *TEKASH* (CRADLE BOARD)

Coyote was traveling upriver, and he was going there. It was a warm spring day, and he grew tired after going upriver only a bend and a half. So he told himself, "I will stop and rest." He lay on the slope just above Lapwai Creek and tried to nap. Soon something was itching him on his elbow, so he rubbed his elbow and brushed it off. Coyote tried to nap again, but the elbow itched again, so he scratched harder on his elbow. The third time, he sat up and scratched very hard, and the elbow got sore. Coyote scratched until he felt something moving on his elbow; he looked, and something fell on the ground.

Now at this time Coyote couldn't have kids because he had been traveling the world and had been too busy doing his work. So he never had kids.

Coyote looks down on the ground and sees something wiggling like a worm. "*Unah!* It's a *miyapkawit* [mee-yap-ka-wit; newborn baby]! Oh, it's a baby! It's a baby!" He said this over and over again.

Then he looked closer and saw that it was a boy. He said, "I have a son! I have a son!" Coyote was very proud of his son. Then Coyote said, "How will I take care of my son?" He thought awhile. He decided that he needed a *tekash* to put his son in. So he looked around and saw a large flat stone lying near where he was resting. Coyote picked up the stone and made a cradle board. He fed and cared for his son. He sang a song to the boy: "*Hacwal, hacwal, hewes. Hacwal, hacwal, hewes* [hac-wal hac-wal he-wes; Boy, boy, it is. Boy, boy it is]." Coyote happily sang this song over and over again while caring for his son.

Tragically, the baby boy became ill and Coyote couldn't make the baby well. Soon the baby died. Coyote cried, and said to himself, "How will the human beings know I had a son? I know, I'll bury him on the ridge so that when the people go up and down the river they will look up and see my first son there." That's all!

This Coyote story and many related landmarks have been destroyed or partially destroyed by railroads, highways, and towns throughout Nez Perce County over the years. As these landmarks disappear or are destroyed by development, the stories will fade away.

THE YOUNG BOY

It was the month of Wilu pup (we-loo-pup; January), when the air is still cold but soon Alatamal (ah-lah-tah-mal; February) will come, and the root *wii eem* (we-eem; Indian celery) will start to grow on the warm slopes around Lapwai. The Chinook winds will come from the south and west where the Chinook salmon people live along the Columbia River. These warm winds will drive away the stinging cold of winter. As the boy listened to the three old men, the air was still cold. The boy had just had a birthday according to the white man's calendar. His birthday was January 2, 1895. He was born in Nez Perce County at the headwaters of Cottonwood Creek above Culdesac, Idaho, to Eloosilikasit (John) and Zhana (Elizabeth) Pinkham. His father, known as John Pinkham, was born on Alpowa Creek below Clarkston, Washington, in 1860. John is a member of Tomusuh's (Chief Timothy's) band. Elizabeth was born on Asotin Creek close to Asotin, Washington, and a member of Apaswahayqt's (Chief Flint Necklace's) band.

The recent twentieth-century census of Indian people (required by the Dawes Act) and the allotment of land to them demanded that all Nez Perce Indians choose or be given an English name instead of using their own Indian name. John chose the name Pinkham, borrowed from an early settler in Asotin County. John was known for being a survivor of the Nez Perce War of 1877. Elizabeth did not go on the war trail of 1877. Both lost many close relatives and friends in this war. Thus, the boy became known as Alexius "Alex" Michael Pinkham. He was about to hear and meet great men who played meaningful roles in the history of the Nez Perce people.

Hinmotuuyalakekt (he-in-mot-to-u-la-kekt; Thunder Rolling Across Lofty Mountains), of 1877 Nez Perce War fame and known to white Americans as Chief Joseph, had just visited the reservation in Idaho and spoke to the young boy Alex. When Joseph was introduced, he asked, "Who are your parents?"

Alex replied, "Eloosilikasit *ka* Zhana."

Joseph said, "*Ehe!* [Yes!] I know your father. He looked after the horses on the war trail. After the Big Hole fight your *tota* was sent back to the Idaho reservation with five young boys, because the soldiers killed children. I know your grandparents. They lived in my country long ago."

Alex described Joseph as a quiet man who could carry on a great dialogue once he started talking. At times Joseph looked sad and troubled, but when engaged in conversation he was joyful. This was Alex's brief meeting with the renowned *miyoxat* (leader).

THE PUPPY INCIDENT

Pakaowna said, "I know the story of the puppy incident that happened with the Soyapo *miyoxat* [white man leader] called Lewis.

This happened at Ciwikite [sa-weet-tah], which is just a short distance from here. The place is on the north side of the Clearwater River and opposite the bluffs, just below where Reverend Spalding was found when he ran away from Walla Walla after Whitman was killed in November 1847. About one mile downriver, on the Blackeagles' allotment, is where it happened. The Blackeagles and Peopeo Tholickt are descendants of Red Bear, who talked with Lewis in 1806. Lewis and Clark were coming back upriver in the time called Ahpahahl [May]. All the time, Lewis and Clark were looking for *hipt* [food], and when they had little or no food they ate dogs and horses. But sometimes they ate *yuc ciqamqal* [pitiable dogs]. Sometimes they were given horses to eat because they looked so *yucna* [poor/pitiful], and we ate horse with them to be polite and good to

This 1931 family photo represents one generation of about thirty to thirty-five years [see Prologue] of a young couple and their children at Ciwikite, where the puppy incident occurred. The author's father, Alex Pinkham (standing on the left), is the grand-nephew of Cut Nose and his mother, Annette Blackeagle-Pinkham (right rear), is a direct descendant of Red Bear. This photo was taken before the author was born into a family of nine.

them. *Ayeaa!* We never ate dogs with them! We never ate dogs because they helped us while tracking and hunting. Like with the horse, you always watched their ears and which way they looked when traveling because it might mean that danger was close or game was near.

"Peopeo Tholickt's grandmother was talked into trading a dog to Lewis, but she reluctantly gave it up. She got ribbon and small items in trade, but later, Red Bear found them to be cheap.

"The grandmother had a daughter, who was Peopeo Tholickt's older relative. The little girl got upset because Lewis and the men were cooking her playmate. A young man, a close relative of Peopeo Tholickt, picked up a little puppy and threw it almost into Lewis's plate, which had dog meat in it.

"This was not play for Lewis. He picked up the puppy, then threw it, hitting the young Nez Perce man in the chest. Then Lewis picked up a tomahawk and motioned to the young man that he just might kill him. The young man retreated quickly after trying to take up the cause of the young girl. Can't make fun with these Soyapo! Their minds don't work right sometimes."

ORDWAY, THE SOYAPO

As the three elder men continued their conversation, each would contribute what they knew about the strange creatures called Soyapo. Panickonee said, "This is what Twisted Hair spoke of many years ago. . . .

"Twisted Hair said that in 1806 three Soyapo of Lewis and Clark's band came from Kamiah to the Pikunen [Snake River] where the Sugunma [Snake River Nez Perce] lived. They had no manners. It was when the *nasoox* [na-so-kh; Chinook salmon] started up the Snake River in May. The leader of the three was called Ordway, and he would peek into lodges, then go right on in uninvited! The *eeyec* [i-yets; women] complained about what he was doing. So Twisted

Hair told the three Soyapo, 'You wait outside this lodge, and we will take you in when we are ready for you.' After a while the three were invited in. They sat down on robes, and a whole cooked salmon was placed before each. They were told to 'eat all you can eat,' so they ate until no more could be eaten by each man. Each man ate only one-fourth of the salmon placed before him. Twisted Hair now said, 'This is how it will be done: you wait, and we invite you in when we are ready for you.'

"Twisted Hair had guided the three from Kamiah to this village in Cougar Bar/Cochrane's Islands on the Snake River. He didn't return with them to their camp on the Clearwater River. Instead he remained at this village because he had many duties to perform and could not leave with them. It was Ke'uyit [kew-u-yet; First Foods Time]. Salmon needed to be divided among the people so everyone got salmon to eat. The salmon were not coming up the river in great numbers yet, and those people who lived a great distance away needed salmon for their village on the prairie and so did the people at the Wallowas. If salmon were waiting to be distributed, they were given out with no explanation needed. This was Ni Mii Puu law. A few freshly caught salmon, which Ordway had traded for, were hanging and were given to people who needed fish. Ordway complained, but no one listened to him. The salmon would probably spoil anyway because it was at least a two-and-a-half-day horseback ride to Kamiah. People needed salmon because few were being caught."

RED BEAR

Pakaowna said, "Let's talk of Xaxaac Illpilp [ha-hots ill-pilp; Red Grizzly Bear or Bloody Grizzly Bear]. He was a powerful *miyoxat,* and he had great power for looking into the future. In later years Red Bear was called Many Wounds because he received eighty wounds and he died at ninety years of age. When Lewis and Clark came to our country, Red Bear was fifty-three years old and a famous great leader of his people. All the tribes knew of his fighting skills, but he was a man of peace also.

"Red Bear wanted to know more of these strange people we called Soyapo. Twisted Hair or his brother and two other Nez Perce went east along the Missouri River and found that these strange people were coming up the river in 1804. The Mandan Indians had them in their winter camp that year. The three Nez Perce gained news of the trade goods and why they were coming west. The Soyapo wanted to find the salt water to the west. While the Nez Perce were there, they traded for two axes that came from the Mandan village. The message from Lewis and Clark was peace and friendship, and a *kitsuy* [coin] had these markings on it with hands clasping. They wanted peace and friendship and no war among all people. This is a good message! This news started a great discussion about Soyapo when the three Nez Perce returned home.

"Red Bear and Twisted Hair had long talks about what we should do when these strange creatures came to our country. Tomusuh [father of Chief Timothy], Cut Nose, and other leaders heard this talk. Some of the Salmon River Tito'oqan [American Indians] wanted to kill these strange people because the prophecies foretold what bad things would happen to the Ni Mii Puu. *'Iyeaa!* The rivers will run red with our blood and these Soyapo will push around and abuse our elders. Our children will be taken away!' they said.

"Others said, 'Look at the things these strange people can do. They can make *kicuy* [kes-ooy; metal] and *qalawn* [kh-la'wn; beads]. They make *timuni* [tee-moo-nee; weapons] that kill at a great distance. We have six of these *timuni*, but we have no black powder which makes them work, and we have no lead balls that kill. Our enemies to the east and north have these *timuni* in great numbers and we don't. What can we do to get these many things that will make our life easier and help us to protect our families better?' So the talks continued way into the night and many points were made, both good and bad, on what to do when these Soyapo came here.

"Finally Red Bear and Twisted Hair said that a choice needed to be selected on what to do. 'We can sit idle and hope everything will be good when the Soyapo come, or we can make peace with our enemies, show the Soyapo we can be peaceful like they want. Then we will be in good with them, and trade can happen with them.' Many agreed, then someone said, 'Let us hear from Watxuuwiis [wat-kh-oo-wees; One Who Is Lost and Returns Home]. She knows of these strange people.'

"Watxuuwiis was an elderly woman who lived up the Clearwater River near a place called Acaga, where the river comes in from the north and many salmon are caught. She was a Ni Mii Puu who was taken prisoner by an eastern Plains tribe while her family was hunting buffalo on the plains. She had been a young girl when captured, and her captors treated her terribly. She suffered many humiliating acts upon her body. As she grew older, her desire to return home became stronger, and one day she made her escape when no one watched her closely. As she traveled, she came upon *silu hix hix* or "white-eyed" people, and she was treated kindly. Watxuuwiis stayed with them awhile, and a white man wanted to take her across the great waters of the East. She somehow made them understand she was going west back to her homeland many, many days' travel away. At this time she had a baby with her as she traveled, but the baby became sick and it died along the way. She buried the baby so the wolves would not get the body. She had been near five great lakes and was now traveling home.

"Watxuuwiis was guided by her spirit helper all the way home. When she arrived, the name meaning 'One Who Is Lost and Returns Home' was given to her in a naming ceremony. Since that time she has been known as Watxuuwiis. She had told this story many times and stated, 'When these strange people come, treat them kindly as they have treated me.' So this story is well known among the Ni Mii Puu. She swayed the argument not to kill these people. She affirmed that her story and great adventure was true. Now the leaders understood what needed to be done, and it was the beginning of a new lifeway and changing times.

"Xaxaac Illpilp [Red Bear] was a talented leader and strong in warfare because he suffered the loss of his parents when he was a young boy. His father, PahWyanan, and two of his wives were going up the Tamanmo [ta-man-mo; Salmon River] when Bannocks surprised and killed them. One of the wives was Red Bear's mother. This happened sometime in the latter part of the 1750s. Red Bear had six sons and many daughters by a Nez Perce wife and a Salish wife. He had strong ties with the Salish people because of this marriage into the tribe. New directions and better relationships with tribes now had to be negotiated and accomplished. Red Bear was determined to be peaceful and friendly with the Shoshone and Bannock people. This would mean a great deal of personal sacrifice and pain to the heart, but he would try to the greatest extent humanly possible, with the help of his family and villagers. He had to think of a way to establish peace with a people who had killed his father and mother many years ago. It was painful to think of what had to be done. It was for all his people that this had to be done. His father's words came to him: 'Do this for your people and there will be joy in your heart.'

"In early 1805, after the snows melted, Red Bear sent one volunteer and two experienced men south to seek peace with the Bannocks. There was a long wait, and the three emissaries failed to return. The summer months passed, and finally word came that the three Ni Mii Puu emissaries had been slain by the Bannocks. The peace mission had failed, and mourning was done for those lost. The discussion was short on what to do next. Fighting men were gathered, weapons made and tested, horses well trained, spirit helpers engaged, and prayers put upon the winds with eagles to carry the messages skyward. The best fighting men were sent south with Red Bear as war leader. The date they left by the white man's calendar was September 17, 1805, three days before Captain William Clark and his party arrived at Weippe Meadows near present-day Wieppe, Idaho. The Ni Mii Puu fighting men had a vengeful mission that they meant to fulfill.

"The war party returned to Acaga (Ahsahka), at the mouth of the north fork of the Clearwater River. The Corps of Discovery were about to finish their canoes and not much notice was given the Nez Perce by Lewis and Clark. But a great honoring ceremony was conducted and concluded for those men deserving such honor because no loss of life occurred among the Nez Perce. Forty-two Tewelka [Enemy to Be Fought] were slain to avenge the deaths of the three previous emissaries. Conflict and discord still existed with the people to the south; this, Red Bear explained to Captain Lewis in May of 1806 near Kamiah, Idaho, while they waited for the snows to melt on the buffalo trail to the east.

"The number of persons dead were one sergeant of the Corps of Discovery (from appendicitis), three Nez Perce emissaries, two Blackfeet killed by Lewis's party near the Maris River in Montana on their return trip in 1806, and forty-two Bannocks. Therefore, the total is forty-eight people killed because of a message of peace and friendship! It is ironic that a message of peace and friendship brought about the spilling of blood to so many people. This was the beginning of the great change that came to Ni Mii Puu country."

EPILOGUE

The history of the Nez Perce has been long and tragic, yet all through these events we have survived the changing times. The dynamic of spirituality and leadership has affected the survival of the people. We asked Lewis and Clark, "Is the earth the mother and the sun the father?" It appears the question was confusing to them because we never got a clear answer, and Red Bear sent members of his family to St. Louis in 1831 to find out more information about the "Book." "Is the Book the Bible or the Book of Knowledge?" The oral rendition of lessons and history I received as a boy were not the Bible, but we sought the ability to read and write, thus learning the technology of the day. Yet many Nez Perce did take up the Bible. It affected the survival of the people but also divided us. So leadership now became a very important factor for the welfare of the Nez Perce.

In 1855 a treaty was concluded at Walla Walla, Washington, with a loss of half the territory of the tribe. Old Joseph dropped the Bible because of the religious factions in conflict over whose religion was best. The social and economic pressures on the tribe brought about more losses of land and sovereignty. The war of 1877 brought about the death of many leaders. Only Young Joseph survived, and he desperately struggled for the well-being of his people. Along with Joseph on the war trail was the son of Captain William Clark, called "Halatookit" (hah-lah-too-kit; Daytime Smoker), his presence having been conceived by Red Bear's daughter as an alliance-building mechanism. This hereditary linkage did not work. Halatookit died while in exile in Oklahoma at the age of seventy-one years, virtually unnoticed by white society.

The historical reference to three generations of Nez Perce was depicted by events as they occurred and were etched in the memory of tribal elders. Because we have lost much of our oral traditions, a great deal of historical detail has been lost. I and retired Northwest-history professor Dr. Steven R. Evans have found some details in brief written accounts by tribal members who had the foresight to record them. As a young boy I listened to my father, Alex M. Pinkham, retell those many prophecies he heard from the three old men as they sat in the long tent. I also received reminders from my siblings on what we heard from our father. History has not been kind to the Nez Perce, but we are still here in our homeland. We have social and economic problems to this day, and we are solving those on a day-by-day basis.

The following is an example of confiscation of cultural patrimony. This pictured stone is Coyote's son's cradle board and has been represented in this manner since 1923.

Coyote's son is buried on the ridgeline to the rear and right of the photo. The inscription on the stone reads:

1836

SITE OF THE LAPWAI MISSION
THE FIRST HOME
THE FIRST SCHOOL AND THE
FIRST CHURCH IN IDAHO

ESTABLISHED BY
REV. HENRY HARMON SPALDING
AND
ELIZA HART SPALDING

TABLET PLACED BY THE
IDAHO DAUGHTERS OF THE
AMERICAN REVOLUTION

1923

Coyote's Cradle Board is seen here after it was relocated from the nearby hillside to the right and rear of this photo. It is the upright stone located to the left of the road near the large tree. The DAR set it here in 1923, and it appears the DAR was unaware of the stone's significance to the oral and literary culture of the Nez Perce. The author's father, Alex Pinkham, would lament this action into his aging years by saying, "Oh, they used Coyote's Cradle Board for Spalding's monument!"

Five generations have passed, and in my estimation the Nez Perce people have recovered from the onslaught of the Soyapo. It has been a heavy toll we have had to pay, but leadership and the belief that a better day is coming has sustained us as a people. Some of the last words from our father, Alex: "*There is a day coming. If we do things right, that day will be slowed down; if we do things wrong that day will be speeded up. That day is Judgment Day!*"

Waco qalo! That's all!

I wish to thank two staff members of the Nez Perce National Historic Park (NPNHP) located at Spalding, Idaho: Mr. Robert Applegate, archivist, and Ms. Diana Mallickan, an interpretive specialist, in the park's museum. Both gave assistance willingly.

I received encouragement and assistance from retired Northwest-history professor Dr. Steven R. Evans, who, with his wife, Connie, resides in Lapwai, Idaho. I thank them both.

Lastly, I thank Mr. Alvin M. Josephy, Jr., for our discussions about the Indian perspective on tribal histories and events that changed our world. He agreed that Indian people need to write their own histories and stories, which are of great interest to them.

THE CEREMONY AT NE-AH-COXIE

Roberta and Richard Basch

ROBERTA BASCH, Puyallup and Coeur D'Alene, is a longtime educator and tribal administrator, with a master's in public administration and a B.A. in business administration from the University of Washington, Seattle. Throughout her married life, sharing four children with her husband, Richard, Ms. Basch has earned multiple awards for her community and educational efforts. She has held positions, among others, as tribal executive for the Puyallup Tribe; Indian Education evaluation specialist at Gonzaga University, Spokane, Washington; and faculty member of the Graduate Education Program, Antioch University, Seattle.

RICHARD BASCH, Clatsop Nehalem, is a member of the tribe on whose doorstep the Corps of Discovery arrived in November 1805, and whose hospitality it enjoyed that winter. Unfortunately, the tribe did not benefit, but suffered much thereby. With a B.S. degree from the University of Oregon, and graduate studies at the University of Washington in Seattle and Western Washington University, Basch has been an educator and tribal administrator most of his professional working life. He has had a special connection to the commemoration of the Lewis and Clark expedition through his service as American Indian Liaison with Corps of Discovery II, the exhibit sponsored by the National Park Service and the Lewis and Clark National Historic Trail. Basch achieved a special honor when, in January 2003, representing the Clatsop and Nehalem Tribes, he offered a blessing at the inauguration of the National Park Service's Tent of Many Voices in Monticello, Virginia.

THE CEREMONY AT NE-AH-COXIE

As I was taught, O Sacred Ones, I have come here this good day to form a relationship with you, that my life would be blessed and that I should live like one in your presence. That I should talk to you as I would my grandparents, whom I was also taught to honor and respect with all my heart. So as I am sitting here facing the vast ocean, I find myself in the midst of your beauty. I see a woodpecker flying down and landing only fifteen feet away. I notice it must be the same kind of bird I found lying on the side of the highway only months earlier between Seaside and Warrenton. It was mostly orange with a brown-speckled belly. It sees me now and is staring directly at me. I wonder what it is saying. I can't tell. It decides I can't understand him and goes about its business pecking at the ground.

Remember, Great Spirit, I used that woodpecker's feathers I found to send off prayers to you from the highest mountain. Today I thank you for bringing me that woodpecker and, moreover, for blessing the prayer I made on that good day. What a beautiful morning it is, the warm summer breeze pressing gently across my skin. I appreciate the vast beauty and the smell of the salty ocean, and the morning dew covering the beautiful green ferns and Oregon grapes. I also enjoy the smell rising upward from the pine needles and the moss lying inches thick below me. I see the dark spot almost fully hidden by time, where my husband, Dick, and our daughters, Charlotte and Lorraine, and our good friend and neighbor Chris held our most powerful ceremony in your honor to bring the power of the ancient ones back to this land.

I remember Charlotte said this ceremony was the most beautiful one she'd ever been a part of. I remember watching her in the light of the sacred fire as she looked into the darkness underneath the veil of pine trees as if watching butterflies float through the air. Her face was more bright and beautiful than I had ever seen. I glanced at Lorraine, who wore an intense face ever so focused on the prayer I was in the middle of.

As you remember, Ancient Ones, I was praying that you, and the ancestors of this land, would come to us if you would want to help these good people here, the Clatsops. The people who lived here for thousands of years. I called the spirits who waited patiently for this day to arrive, Chief Tostow, Tickahah, Dunkal, and all the other great ones of 1851 who signed the Tansy Point Treaty between the Clatsops and the United States government. This treaty was to have established a reservation at what is now called Fort Stevens State Park, giving the tribe permanent fishing grounds at the mouth of the Ne-ah-coxie River, and annual payments. These good people signed this treaty in good faith, knowing their time had come. The spirits are talking to me from a time long ago. They are telling me about their Celiast: "Our relative, she now lives with them, and believes in their God. And our lands have been overrun by them. Our people are dying of diseases that our ceremonies cannot cure. Too few, too sick."

I then recalled a letter I had read, written by Robert Shortess, the acting subagent of Indian Affairs of that time in 1843. Shortess reported to his superiors that Clatsop Indian lands and fishing stations were taken over, and that the Clatsop Indians had been threatened with the vengeance of the government if they opposed in any manner the encroachment of the settlers. He said that the Clatsops were told that they might as well give up their lands for what payment they could get, since the soldiers were coming to kill them or drive them off and that it was in vain for them to oppose the whites for they would take their land in defiance of them. He reported that aged and infirm Indians and orphan children were in a state of destitution and suffering. He asked if there was a way in which a check could be put upon the encroachment of individuals upon Indian territory. He wondered if every white man had a right to take their land where and how they pleased, and wondered if the home government had no will or their agents in Oregon no power to protect the Clatsops. He said that the Clatsop Indian property was constantly passing from them. He reported that disease and death were the consequences of contact with whites. Their houses and the bones of their deceased ancestors and relatives had been violated and burnt. The spontaneous production of the earth and the crops that they had planted had been destroyed by the stock of settlers, and they were treated as aliens and intruders in their own country. He remarked that in a few years more disease and death would have done its work on the "Redman of Oregon," and they would have dispersed from the face of the earth. He questioned whether our government was aware of this fact and was waiting for its consummation. He pleaded that something should be done about it immediately; justice and honor demanded it.

I remembered the first time I saw Joe Scovell, a small man most noticeably of coastal Indian stature. I was touched by his gentleness. His skin was dark, almost as dark as mine. He had a quiet earnestness about him that I now understand. Although he is now eighty-two years old, he gives pretty close to 100 percent of his waking hours to the life of his tribes, the Clatsops and Nehalems of the most northern coast of Oregon. His wife, Maecel, says that his work for his people is about all he does. He has found that there is so much to do, yet so little time in the day. And there is so little time in his life to unravel the mistake made by history and to make it right.

I prayed that night, Great Spirit, that all that was made wrong be made right. I acknowledged that progress comes from the nature of life, and nothing can or should interrupt the natural phenomena of change. But I also acknowledged, Great Spirit, that the vessels of change are sometimes damaged, dirty, tainted. They come in the form of mankind. And in that particular time, one man in particular, my ancestor, the renowned John McLoughlin, the head benefactor of the Hudson's Bay Company, held no compassion for these good people of this land. I found myself ashamed to say that I am a direct descendant of McLoughlin, and that my daughter Lorraine once held the name McLoughlin. But I learned more about him, about how he cared more about the cargo on his ships than the people who manned them; about how in 1829, a ship, the *William and Ann*,

was wrecked and lost its cargo, and the Clatsops, who lived on the
south shore of the mouth of the Columbia River and called their
home Ne-ah-keluc (referred to as Point Adams by early fur traders
and pioneers and now known as Fort Stevens), found the cargo and
kept it. For many years before Lewis and Clark arrived in 1805, the
Indians all along the coast found objects washed ashore from passing ships from Europe, Russia, and Asia, and kept them. My husband,
Richard, or Dick, as we call him, has stories about them, including
one about his family finding a wooden trunk, once filled with
beeswax, which he still owns. But something was different in 1829.
My ancestor, John McLoughlin, demanded that this particular cargo
be returned. According to the elders of that time, when the Clatsops
didn't return the items, McLoughlin ordered the village to be
attacked, and many tribal people, not only in the village that had the
cargo but in many nearby villages, were killed, including many of
the chiefs as well as tribal members.

Dick and I changed Lorraine's name from Lorraine McLoughlin
Basch to Lorraine Nina Basch. Lorraine, after my deceased beautiful,
strong-willed sister with the best laugh in the world; and Nina, after
my sister-in-law, a loving soul with laughter and wit. In this way our
beautiful daughter Lorraine could live without being tainted, and
bring goodwill to our current times.

We named our older daughter, Charlotte, Charlotte Celiast Basch,
in honor of the great Clatsop Chief Cobaway's daughter, Celiast, and
her daughter Charlotte. And both women, like Chief Coboway, were
honored, respected, and remembered with the highest regard. Not
only by their Clatsop people, but by the pioneers who settled in their
homelands as well, and who wrote about them in their history. Lewis
and Clark also gave me an idea about how Coboway conducted his
life. I remember, Great Spirit, reading what they wrote about
Coboway only twenty-three years before McLoughlin attacked
Coboway's village. They said that they had found the most friendly

and decent Indians they had met within this neighborhood. The neighborhood of the Clatsops. And on March 22, 1806, the Lewis and Clark expedition gave Fort Clatsop to Chief Coboway, writing these words: "He has been much more kind and hospitable to us than any other Indian in this neighborhood." Lewis and Clark reported that the Clatsops in general were polite, friendly, and very neat, and cleaned themselves quite often.

Great Spirit, what a coincidence that after more than 150 years Dick Basch, great-great-great-grandson of Coboway, and I, great-great-great-granddaughter of Dr. John McLoughlin, would marry and relive history together. Our families trace back to separate places and separate lives before we met. And now we find how closely our family's lives came together in history. My grandmother, who was proud to say she was the great-granddaughter of John McLoughlin, was part Kootenai and part Irish. She was always proud of her Irish background. She even sang Irish songs with a beautiful voice and an Irish accent. She spoke often of the "little people," the leprechauns. My

Celiast Coboway Smith, ca. 1830.
Basch family photograph.

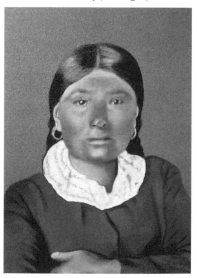

Charlotte Smith and her brother Silas Smith,
around 1885. Basch family photograph.

mother and father also talked of the little people. We called them Stick Indians. They were different from the leprechauns who owned the pot of gold. Stick Indians were tricksters who often stole things and were known to most Indian tribes from Oregon to Alaska. And just when you thought you'd never see a stolen object again, it would miraculously be returned. Stick Indians do this just to be a bother.

My Kootenai-Irish grandmother married a full-blooded Coeur d'Alene Indian from Idaho, Nicholas Campbell, and had four daughters, one of them, my mother, Elaine Briden. My father, Reuben Wright, is a full-blooded Puyallup from Washington State, where I met Dick. At first, I had no idea Dick was Indian at all because he was much taller than most coastal Indians—six feet, six inches tall. His skin was lighter. Yet his mannerisms were like ours. He had respect for every word that was spoken to him. He lent himself to helping our elders and made himself available to learn from them. About our mother Earth, beliefs, practices, traditions. He seemed to be an honorable person, quite friendly and patient. He also gave to the children of our tribe, for the elders hired him to help start a school for their grandchildren. When I first read how Lewis and Clark described Coboway and the Clatsops, I thought about when I met Dick. When I watch our daughters, Lorraine and Charlotte, now growing into young women, the way they hold themselves with dignity, with traditional regalness, I think of Coboway's daughter, Celiast.

Oh, what a coincidence, Great Spirit, that you would bring our families back together again. I believe you did this to help make things right. I remember the piece of china Dick told me about after we were engaged and first found out about our families' histories in common. His ancestor Celiast married her second husband, Solomon Smith, in 1841. Solomon worked as a teacher for John McLoughlin at the Hudson's Bay Company in Vancouver after the Hudson's Bay Company moved their headquarters to Fort Vancouver from Astoria. As a wedding gift, John McLoughlin gave them a china set, and only one piece remains after more than 150 years. It passed from Celiast's hands to her daughter Charlotte and then to Dick's mother, Winifred.

O Great Spirit, you made our mothers happy that day when our families came together again! I only wish my Kootenai-Irish grandmother, Margaret O'Sullivan-Campbell, could have lived to hear the tale and see this keepsake. Since then, Winifred passed away, as you know, Great Spirit, and now this piece of china belongs to Dick and me. And although she left us, her love, her stories, her beliefs, and her mannerisms live on to this day.

Our daughter Charlotte said she saw her grandma, whom we called Winn, that night during the ceremony above the fire. She said her heart was filled by the love she felt when her grandma held her in her arms and smiled gently into her eyes. Winn looked very much like her grandmother Charlotte Smith, Celiast's daughter. Her face was shaped the same, and Dick has heard many times that she held herself with the same regalness that both Celiast and her daughter Charlotte had.

Winn lived with us until she was close to death. Dick worried for years about how to bury his mother with her family in the Clatsop Plains Pioneer Cemetery, which over the years had become an official historic landmark and closed to further burials. Dick remembers going with his mom to that cemetery as long ago as when he was a small child. She would pack in dirt or sand from the beach to fill in the graves as they sank deeper into the ground. She would pick out the weeds and manicure the graves with her bare hands, paying extra-special attention to who was buried where and telling each of their stories. Celiast, Charlotte, Silas. Silas was Celiast's son, and he became a successful attorney who represented the Clatsops in one of their first land claims. Later he became an honored member of Oregon's legislature, as well as a valued historian. This cemetery is beautiful. It is more like a peaceful park than a cemetery. It is part of the first church established in the Oregon territory, the Pioneer Presbyterian Church. The cemetery lies, for the most part undisturbed and forgotten, on what was once sand dunes, now grown over by grass and a few towering trees. On the last and highest ridge, just before a beautiful lively stream, there is a huge tree that somebody years ago tied a rope to, and that our children swing on when we visit and manicure the graves.

Thank you, Great Spirit, for the good luck you gave to Dick and Winn. I remember when she turned ninety years old. Dick again took up the cause that he and his brother, Jerry, started ten years earlier to get the Clatsop County Board of Commissioners to overrule a policy that would not allow Winn to be buried with her Indian family in that historic pioneer cemetery.

At the time, we lived on my reservation in Washington State. Dick drove regularly to Astoria several times a month, volunteering his time and giving his knowledge to the organizers of the two hundredth commemoration of the Lewis and Clark expedition. During that year he met many people who knew about Dick's ancestry because of Coboway and Celiast's history in common with the Lewis and Clark expedition. Many of them came to help him as he prepared to meet the commissioners in person for the first time.

Since the commissioners' upcoming meetings were advertised, people throughout the area found out that Dick's heart was set on changing the commissioners' minds about their previous decision to deny Winn the right to be buried with her family. Radio stations aired information about his endeavor. Local and national newspapers wrote about him and Winifred, the direct descendant of Coboway, his daughter, Celiast, and all the rest of the family. O Great Spirit, it turned out to be quite the spectacle! I was sitting in our tribal clinic way up north in Washington State when somebody approached me and said that she had read about Dick and his mom in a national Indian newspaper. People made personal calls to the local radio stations and to the commission from all over the country.

As Dick, our daughter Charlotte, and I quietly approached the huge wooden doors of the courthouse, we could hear the sound of our shoes echo throughout the marble corridor. At the other end we noticed a handsome dark Indian man with long, thick black braids, wearing a black hat and a brightly colored Pendleton coat. Since we were the topic of the commissioner's agenda that night, we knew he was there for us, so we introduced ourselves. He said he was from the Warm Springs Tribe, up the Columbia River. He saw an article about the whole thing in a newspaper in the city of Portland and decided to drive the 130 miles down the Columbia to help. He was very quiet, very dignified. He spoke eloquently and with an Indian accent. The commissioners' usual meeting place was changed to this huge ominous space because with all the publicity they expected many visitors that night. Along with Dick's friends from the various Lewis and Clark commemoration planning groups there were others whom he hadn't met who were from local historical societies and newspapers. As you know, Great Spirit, before we arrived Dick prayed for your help with his words that night, because Dick has never liked talking in front of large groups.

Dick was asked to come forward to make his request. As he began to speak his face turned bright red. His voice quivered with emotion under the pressure. He began by telling them about his dying mother and her stories of her grandmother Charlotte, her great-grandmother

Celiast, and Chief Coboway, about their time in history. Suddenly the past opened and we all sat in the middle of the 1800s.

Celiast was born in 1801. She lived to see her father, the great and hospitable Chief Coboway, lead his people with gentleness, intellect, and wisdom; receive respect and be chosen by Lewis and Clark to receive Fort Clatsop as a gift; and later lose his power, authority, and respect in succumbing to a new order. A new order led by Alexander Henry, head of the fur-trading North West Company and backed up by Dr. John McLoughlin and the many pioneers who followed. Celiast transformed externally from the daughter of a great and well-respected tribal leader living in a plank-house village to the wife of a pioneer teacher, yet her heart and soul lived in the Clatsop world. And as she grew older, after her husband died, she again spoke only Clatsop and relayed her culture, her mannerisms, her regalness through the stories she told her son, Silas, and her other children. Silas wrote fondly of his mother in many documents; all the while the continued inflow of pioneers left Celiast's people destitute by the time she died in 1891.

Dick explained how he and his mother and father would go to the cemetery to take care of it together. I felt Winn's beliefs, her heart, her spirit pour throughout the marble room, echoing ever so strongly throughout the ages. Dick told them that he realized the Clatsop Plains Pioneer Cemetery was for pioneers only. A monument to the past, a monument not made of stone, but rather of relationships. And his mother was still very much a part of these relationships. He explained that his mother lived all her life knowing she'd be buried there with her family, never separated by time. The people in that cemetery were people she loved and deeply considered her family, and to her, this cemetery was never a monument. He told them his mother was dying now and didn't know that the county commissioners had previously decided not to allow her burial there in that cemetery, with her family. And because of this, she also didn't know that we were asking them to change their minds and permit her to be buried there in her homeland, with her people, when she passed.

Only then did I notice the tears that streamed down Dick's face. In a silent pause, and with great humbleness, he motioned that this was all that he had to say. He then introduced our daughter Charlotte Celiast Basch and told them she was named after those special people in the cemetery, her relatives Celiast, daughter of Coboway, and her daughter, Charlotte Smith. They asked anybody else if they had anything to say, and some people did, but the man from Warm Springs I remember well. He stood there upright, so powerful, so strong, yet so gentle and peaceful. His presence spoke much more than his words, which were that he asked the good commissioners of this land to honor an old lady's request to be buried with her people, as it was the good and honorable thing to do.

The commissioners then asked technical questions, such as "If we approve your request would we be opening up this opportunity for anybody who wanted to be buried in the pioneer cemetery?" And "Are you going to ruin the landscape when you bury her by bringing in the casket on a truck that would leave tire marks?" After we answered their questions to their satisfaction, one of them scorned us about some of the calls they had received from our supporters, but in the end, they all agreed to let Winn be buried with her family in that pioneer cemetery. At which point the tension in the room was released into a quiet appreciation and silent pleasure.

Before we left, we said our farewells to the man from Warm Springs, who said Winn would pass quickly now that her spirit knew she had a place to go. As we drove away from the courthouse that dark, wet, cold, and windy night, Dick's father called and said Winn was dying and Dick should come home quickly. She passed away quietly with Dick asleep at her side, in the Christmas season of the year 2000, when she was ninety years old, the same age as Celiast when she passed on. Leaving Dick with her heart, her memories, her mannerisms, and her love.

We held a combined Christian and Native ceremony run by both a Presbyterian minister and by the man from Warm Springs at the historic landmark of the region's first Presbyterian church and pioneer cemetery, in Warrenton, Oregon, as was Dick's mom's wish. She was buried with her most treasured possessions, as is our traditional custom. Our daughter Lorraine sat quietly as our sons, Chris and Mike, held their sister, our daughter Charlotte, really close as she cried out loud for her grandmother and said her last good-bye.

We made many small vacation trips back to Dick's family home that year to manicure the graves, swing from the rope tied to the big tree, play on the beaches, and swim in the ocean. Our son Mike loves the ocean. Just like Winn did. Our niece Julie said she remembered her grandmother swimming and playing in the ocean when Winn was seventy years old and thought that all grandmothers were like her at that age. When Mike suggested we move to Seaside, we jumped on it.

When we first moved to Seaside, I was sad to see nothing of Indian people in the area, or in the Seaside Historical Society Museum. I saw many, many old photos of blond-haired tourists in really old-time swimming suits flocked on the beaches, and relics from the logging era. But no presentations of Indian history. I was even sadder to see a framed copy of a very old news article romantically claiming that the woman in its accompanying picture was one of the "Last of the Clat-sops," Jenny Michell, sitting in front of her cedar-planked house, preparing cedar and grass for her next basket; I saw this on the wall of a pizza parlor. A curiosity piece for the tourists. I was alone. The only dark, nearly full-blooded Indian around. A little boy in our daughters' school called me a black lady. People here were just not used to seeing Indians.

After all of Winn's stories, where did all the Indians go? I remember, Great Spirit, when I found my morning prayer spot. I wondered, Did the ancient people from here pray like me? Were they still here? Now I know from a document I read entitled *The Centennial History of Oregon*, which refers throughout to works by our relative Silas Smith, Celiast's son, that they knew you, Great Spirit. They knew you, Grandmother Ocean, Mother Earth, and Father Sun! And unfortu-nately, I found that they were also mocked and ridiculed for believ-ing as I do now. Even though the signs you gave them through nature were proven to be true.

I prayed about my sadness. About how these good people of

Winn's stories appeared to be gone. Had they really all died? Only one piece of memory left in a pizza parlor? I remember praying, "If this is not the case, O Great Spirit, let us see them." And as you would remember, Great Spirit, you brought them together for me to see. Oh, what a joy that was for Dick to receive a phone call from Joe Scovell, chairman of the Clatsop-Nehalem Tribe. Even that was nearly unbelievable. As you know, Dick and Joe talked for hours, discovering that they had met twenty years prior in a tiny village in Alaska, where Dick went to help him with questions about the federal government's program to help Indians through their Indian Education Program.

After their long phone call and a good visit, Great Spirit, you revealed that many of the Clatsops were still alive. They may have been crowded out, forgotten, shoved aside, but they were alive. Soon after Dick and Joe shared their histories and reconnected as close relatives, we started going to the Clatsop-Nehalem Confederated Tribal meetings and found many other families that shared our ancestry, our histories, and our dreams. Although few, they had stayed together in small groups in small communities, after most of the Indians from the North Coast of Oregon had moved to nearby reservations, where they became recognized as Indians by joining other tribes and were protected by an officially signed U.S. treaty, or they had integrated into the white culture. During that time, according to ethno-historian Dr. Doug Deur, while other tribes were granted treaties, there was no official removal process established by the United States to move Clatsops and Nehalems from this particular area to other reservations. These people loved their homelands, and many refused to uproot their families. They didn't want to move, and now they barely survive. These are the tiny handful who lived through smallpox, venereal diseases, slaughters like the one imposed by Dr. John McLoughlin, unratified treaties, pioneers, loggers, fishermen, and cattlers.

After nearly two hundred years since the Lewis and Clark expedition passed through, and so many atrocities, how could this tiny handful survive? Why them? They must be here for some very important reason, Great Spirit. They all know you, Great Spirit, Mother

Earth, Father Sun, four-legged and winged ones. They all appreciate and cherish the beauty and power of the great Oregon coast. For some really good reason you must have saved their lives, their spirit, their histories, their knowledge, and their good hearts. And as I watch them my heart heaves up a great sadness for them. O Great Spirit, don't let these good people disappear. Oh, please don't let them die. Let them be honored in their own country, live under their own name. Don't let them be known only as history, a picture in a pizza parlor. Their good hearts are what this world needs right now. Their bright smiles, their generosity, their friendship, their kindness, their respect toward our Mother Earth, their laughter.

Oh, Great Spirit, I am sorry for my ancestor John McLoughlin. I stand here in his place this good day and ask for you to forgive him and all those who hurt these good people.

As I did in our great ceremony on the most beautiful place on earth, Ne-ah-coxie, a former Clatsop village whose name means "small pine trees," the place now referred to as the Seaside Gateway, the traditional Clatsop fishing grounds where the Necanicum, Neawana, and Neacoxie rivers join together and flow as one into our grandmother Ocean, who is only a few hundred feet away; the place where Celiast and her family returned home by canoe from the long journey that took her first to Fort George, now known as Astoria, where she married a man who worked for the Hudson's Bay Company and with whom she had two children, and then on to Fort Vancouver, where her husband became abusive to her and left her alone and heartbroken when Dr. McLoughlin sent him away with her children to Canada to live with the wife he already had; and from French Prairie near Portland, where she lived with her second husband, Solomon Smith, a former teacher from the Hudson's Bay Company; this place, where her people, the Clatsops, were so happy to see her come home that they didn't wait for her and her family to paddle ashore, but ran out into the water and lifted Celiast and each of her family members up by their haunches and carried them on their shoulders to the beach where they had a huge feast; this same place, where I sit now; I can vaguely see and hear their voices to this day;

this beautiful place preserved by the good people who call themselves the North Coast Land Conservancy; this place, the most beautiful place on earth; again, I ask you, Great Spirit, please bless these good people.

I remember, Great Spirit, when Neal from the Land Conservancy brought Dick and me here for the first time since Dick's return home. As we approached this place, I smelled sweetgrass and felt light, so light I felt as if I could float. I could hear a song. I said out loud to both Dick and Neal that I could feel that a ceremony had been held there and that they had used sweetgrass in the ceremony, a ceremony that was usually held by Indians of the plains area. Neal explained that there was a ceremony held here by the family of Reuben Snake, a medicine man of the Winnebago Tribe, a Green Beret, the first president of the American Indian Movement, a former chairman of the Winnebago Tribe of Nebraska, which is now located on the Lewis and Clark Trail, past president of the National Congress of American Indians, and roadman of the Native American Church. He also led the effort to overturn the U.S. Supreme Court case *Employment Div., Oregon Dept. of Human Resources v. Smith* in 1990, thus securing the federal legislation called the American Indian Religious Freedom Act Amendment of 1994, which protects the dignity and future use of Indian tools and methods for Indian religious practices. And, O Great Spirit, what a coincidence that Reuben, from Nebraska, would be involved in a case emerging from Oregon and would have a monument in his honor placed here in Ne-ah-coxie. A man who was healed by Reuben Snake bought this land in honor of Reuben and gave it to the Land Conservancy, and Reuben's family held a ceremony in Reuben's honor because he passed away before he could see it.

Remember, Great Spirit, in our ceremony that night we called out to you to forgive what was done to the good people of this land. We asked that you take this treaty that was signed in good faith by these good people but never ratified by the Congress of the United States, and let the agreements describing and sanctifying the Clatsops' livelihood in their traditional living, hunting, fishing, food-gathering, and spiritually sacred places be honored. We held this treaty up to you and asked for your blessing of it before we threw it into the fire. We stood there with great hope, and deep sorrow, watching the edges of the white paper turn black, then a full, bright flaming red as it danced joyously on the wings of the smoldering gray ashes where it was released up high to the bright stars of the heavenly deep blue night on its way into the spirit world.

And now, Great Spirit, I cry out to you again with this prayer. This is a big prayer, I know, but you see, Great Spirit, these were and are Great People. Let them not be the ones who die in the honor of Lewis and Clark. They are the people who honored and helped them when they finally reached their journey's destination, cold, hungry, and tired. Let them live.

Hey, Great Spirit, four years after Winn's death, I acknowledge there has been a resurgence of the Clatsop people, that the residents of the cities here, those who are archaeologists and historians, have placed artifacts they have uncovered from Clatsop villages on display in their museums, in safekeeping and in goodwill, and that they now know that the Clatsops have survived. I acknowledge that the canoe stolen by Lewis and Clark has been returned after two hundred years in the form of a grant to build a new one. I acknowledge that Dick, whose great-great-great-grandfather Coboway was given Fort Clatsop, now works there and has a key to the front door.

But hey, Great Spirit, these artifacts that the museums have are not artifacts for historical markers and relics of the past; they are alive and should be in the homes of the relatives who live on today. And this canoe we are building does not replace the original one stolen by Lewis and Clark; it is one granted for the purpose of commemorating the two hundred years since Lewis and Clark documented an economic passageway through an already inhabited continent for the then president of the United States, Thomas Jefferson. It is because of this history that these Clatsop people are now few in number. Still living without a treaty, unrecognized by the U.S. government. And although they live and continue to honor you and appreciate the beauty of Mother Earth and all her mysteries, they own

*Charlotte Celiast and Lorraine Nina Basch
at a festival, with their father, Richard,
at right in the background.*

nothing, no land, not even their sacred places of prayer or their ancestors' handmade tools, clothing, utensils, and canoes. Help them, Great Spirit!

Oh please, if anything, let their honor and generosity live. I pray that their treaty will be honored, that they can remain here on these homelands. If not, Great Spirit, they would continue to be absorbed into the mainstream, move to nearby reservations, and lose their identity. Let them keep their name, their culture, their mannerisms, in their own country, in their own homelands. Let not this prayer be the last cry from a once great nation; let it be a call for rebirth. Please, Great Spirit, let them come back and flourish. Great Spirit, I have prayed many prayers in my lifetime, but this one I pray not for me, but for all of us. For those who traveled by foot to Oregon, and the thousands who followed and live in the Clatsops' original homelands. For the Clatsops and Nehalems who live here still and hold a most powerful relationship with you and this land and respect it with their highest regard. For all the nations of Indian people who have suffered and lost. I pray for their good being, for their survival. I pray that they will flourish, and that they will live another day to pass on the good teachings they still have to offer. Let them not disappear. We would never wish ill against progress. Only to make things right. O Great Spirit, bless this prayer this good day.

THE VOICES OF ENCOUNTER

N. Scott Momaday

N. SCOTT MOMADAY is Kiowa by blood, and poet, painter, playwright, professor, novelist, and storyteller in the flesh. One of America's most distinguished men of letters, Momaday is a winner of the Pulitzer Prize (for the novel *House Made of Dawn*), a Guggenheim Fellow, and a Fellow of the American Academy of Arts and Sciences, and he holds thirteen honorary degrees from colleges and universities from the University of New Mexico to Yale to Blaise Pascal University in France. His many books have been translated into French, German, Italian, Russian, Swedish, Japanese, and Spanish. He has lectured and given readings around the world and was the first professor to teach American literature at the University of Moscow (1974), where he continues to visit regularly. Recently, he has been focusing his creative efforts on painting and graphic arts, as well as writing.

Momaday resides in Jemez Springs and Santa Fe, New Mexico, where he is a senior scholar at the School of American Research and teaches at the Institute of American Indian Arts. He is the founder and chairman of the Buffalo Trust, a nonprofit foundation for the preservation and restoration of Native American culture and heritage, and was named an Artist for Peace by UNESCO in 2003.

THE VOICES OF ENCOUNTER

I am Lightning Crow of the Arikara. What sort of people would do this? We watched them day by day, as they moved against the winds and rains, the mountains and the rocks. They were few, and they seemed very small against the great land and the great sky. But they moved on, and we watched them. They must have had good medicine. And they must have been looking for more, the best and most powerful of medicines. Yes, it must be so. And this we could understand, for we too move against hunger and hardship to secure our medicine. We quest after visions. I believe that these strangers were on a vision quest.

Children . . . you will have nothing to fear, because the great spirit will smile upon your nation and in future ages will make you outnumber the trees of the forest.

> I am Holyhorn of the Mandan,
> And I hold the talking stick.
> Respectfully I speak.
> I speak with my father's voice,
> My grandfather's voice,
> The voice of my brave people.
> Ours is a proud village.
> Our village is alive with words.
> We are at home in our words,
> In the dignity of words,
> In the power of words,
> In the beauty of words,
> In the timelessness of words.
>
> We must speak of origins.
> We must speak of Creation.

North is the house of origin,
Where the sun is pale,
Where the needles of the sun pierce the snow,
And the thin light is brittle and bright.
And behind the light,
In the long night, in utter darkness,
We emerged.
We began to be.
We began to breathe and to see.
We began to see through the darkness.
In our emergence was the dawn,
And we began to see,
And we were dazzled.
Dazzling was the light,
Dazzling was the earth,
Dazzling were the waters,
Dazzling were the leaves and flowers,
Dazzling were the rain and rainbows.
In storms of beauty were we dazzled.
Then the animals emerged,
The bear, the deer, the muskrat,
The porcupine and the mouse.
Then the birds emerged,
The eagle, the raven, the loon,
The magpie and the owl.
Then the fishes emerged,
The salmon, the catfish, the trout,
The steelhead and the carp.
The animals emerged.
And we began to be,
And we began to be in ourselves,
With hands that grasped,
With legs that were long and straight,
With feet that danced on the earth,
With voices that called and sang,

With voices that sang of our becoming,
With voices that sang of our being,
With voices that made a wind of words.
The first word was spoken,
And we cringed to hear it.
The first word was spoken,
And the animals cringed to hear it.
The first word was spoken,
And even the gods cringed to hear it.
For it was the sound of origin and being.
It was the sound of wilderness breathing.
It was the sound of the sun burning.
It was the sound of life and death.
It was the sound that opens the silence is heard.
The sound in which the silence of the stars
All the words of time followed upon it.

And our mouths shaped words,
And our destiny was shaped.
With words we made our sacred songs.
We took possession of language,
And we danced in the river of language,
And our being was borne on words.
Therefore I speak.
I speak of strangers coming.
They were not of our world.
We welcomed them to our world.
We gave them melons.

The Indian halted again and turned his horse about as if to wait for
me . . . When I arrived within about 150 paces I again repeated the
word "tab-ba-bone" and held up the trinkits in my hands and striped up
my shirt sleeve to give him an opportunity of seeing the colour of my
skin, and advanced leasurely towards him.

Sacagawea, as imagined by Glenna Goodacre.
Photograph by James Hart.

I am Sacagawea of the Shoshone. I am a woman of the horse people. I am a woman of the people of the mountains. I am a woman who was taken from my people when I was young. I was taken, and therefore I am a woman of the Mandan. I am Bird Woman. When the white men came I was a girl. I was one of the wives of Charbonneau, a white man, and there was a baby in my belly. I was glad and afraid. Charbonneau said that he was going with the white men. Charbonneau said that I must come with him and with them. I was glad and afraid. I was a captive girl and a young married woman. There was a baby in my belly. They were thirty white men. Charbonneau was a white man. My baby and I were two. Even my baby was half a white man. I was glad and afraid.

I remembered the language of the horse people. The white men wanted me to take them to the horse people and to speak the horse people's language. They wanted me to ask for horses. They were going toward the setting sun. They were going to the water at the end of the land. They were going over high mountains. They had much to carry. They needed horses. I was going with them, over mountains, to the water at the end of the land. I had been gone from the horse people a long time. I did not know where they were. But I wanted to find them. I wanted to taste the words of my first people in my mouth. I wanted to hear the words I first heard. I was glad and afraid.

I thought: I try to help them. I try hard to help them, although I do not understand their purpose. Why do they take such a hard way? I wonder. Why do they fight the hard way and the weather? And why am I with them? Why do I go with them on this hard way? Because I am Charbonneau's wife, and Charbonneau tells me what to do. I am Charbonneau's wife, and I am a good wife. The white men say that I must guide them. They want me to know what I do not know. I have never been beyond the mountains. But I try hard to help them. I am a young woman, and I have a baby in my belly. How can I be of help? The baby is not hard to carry. Maybe this hard way will make the baby a boy. And he will be strong, and he will take long steps, and he will have medicine, and he will take care of his mother and his people. I will make him a beautiful cradle. I will give him good food to eat and my good milk and mountain water to drink. When he comes from my belly he will see the clear dawn and the bright meadows of the mountains, and he will laugh to see the glitter of light upon the waters. He will be a man, a man of the Mandan and the Hidatsa and a man of the Shoshone.

On the hard way I had respect for the white men. They had much strength and courage. Every day they had to fight the hard way. Every step of the hard way was a little victory, a little making of the quest. And I became a part of it. At night, on the hard ground, I dreamed. I dreamed as a warrior dreams. With these men, and with my son, I made a vision quest. I was the woman of the quest. Along the hard way I began to think of myself as Bird Woman, a warrior and the mother of a warrior. I was nearly proud. I thought of myself in a way that women do not think of themselves. I made a song. Every day I made a little more of the song. I kept the song to myself. Perhaps I would give it to my son in time.

We came to a place where we could not go on. We could not go on without horses. But I had dreamed of finding the Shoshone, my people, and so we found them. I found my brother, who had become a chief. We wept together. And horses were given to us, to carry on the quest. That was a powerful thing, and I was powerful in it. The white men said that I must have dreamed the horses into being. Maybe it is so.

At last, as with our last breath, we drew into ourselves the misty air of the great water. The water reached from the land to the sky. There seemed no end to it. For a long time no one could speak, and tears came to our eyes. I tried to get the whole of the quest in my mind, but I could not, for it was larger than my mind. So much had happened, and what happened belonged to the white men and to me. And because of me it happened to my people as well. The quest was well made.

We traveled easily on the way back, for we knew our way. At the Mandan villages I said good-bye to the white men. There, at the parting, were words, and there were silences. The words rose and spun like leaves in the sky. The silences were forever.

They state the Indians to be as numerous on the Columbia river,, which empties into the Pacific,, as the whites in any part of the U.S. They brought a family of the Mandan Indians with them. The winter was very mild on the Pacific.

> I am Twisted Hair of the Nez Perce.
> We had never seen a white man.
> Then they came among us, weak with hunger.
> They came boldly among us, the Nimipu,
> To our rivers which ran with salmon,
> To our meadows thick with camas.
> We looked them over.
> We looked them over.
> They came with pouches of silver.
> They came with weapons of silver.
> They came wearily, with hunger.

Our young men were boastful.
They spoke haughty words of war.
Brave and reckless in their numbers,
They wanted death for the white men.
They wanted the goods and weapons of the white men.
"With the blood of these enemies,
With their guns and goods,
The Nimipu will stand in a high place,
Rich and powerful," they said.
In counsel it was said, and there was smoke,
And there was thoughtful silence.

Then the old woman Watkuweis spoke.
"I was befriended by men like these.
When I was a girl I was stolen by enemies.
Then I was sold to another tribe.
So was my life made hard and bitter,
And I believed that I was lost forever.
Then white men were kind to me,
And I ran away, and I returned to the Nimipu.
It is a bad thing to be lost.
It may be that these men are lost,
That they want only to return to their people.
Be worthy of your blood, and do them no harm.
I am old and dying, and I remember,
I was befriended by men like these."

And the Nez Perce listened and heeded.
For the Nimipu are the best of peoples.
They are made of the blood of the heart.
Therefore, they are brave and strong,
Generous and good. They are the real people.

Children. Know that the great chief who has . . . offered you the hand
of unalterable friendship is the great Chief of the Seventeen Great

Nations of America, whose cities are as numerous as the stars of the heavens, and the people like the grass of your plains cover . . . the wide extended country . . . to where the land ends and the sun rises from the face of the great waters . . . [H]e will serve you and not deceive you.

For all Americans then and now, the journey of Lewis and Clark and the Corps of Discovery was the epic odyssey of the nation's mind and imagination. For the men who entered the unknown and returned, and for those who knew the land and watched from the heart of wilderness, nothing would be the same ever again. It was the most difficult of journeys, marked by extraordinary triumph and defeat. It was in the truest sense a vision quest, and the visions gained were of profound consequence. All that we are, good and bad, was in it.

Grateful acknowledgment is made to the following for permission to reprint previously published material.

Michael Running Wolf and *Bozeman Daily Chronicle:* Excerpt from "Letter to the Editor dated November 2, 2004," by Michael Running Wolf from *Bozeman Daily Chronicle.* Reprinted by permission of the author and *Bozeman Daily Chronicle.*

Mountrail County Record: Excerpt from "Bullseye's story of Sakakawea" from *Van Hook Reporter* (April 2, 1925). Reprinted by permission of the *Mountrail County Record.*

Robert Miller and *We Proceeded On:* Excerpts from an article by Robert Miller from *We Proceeded On* (2004). Reprinted by permission of the author and *We Proceeded On.*

Page 137: Allen V. Pinkham, Sr. © courtesy of the Sears Portrait Studio, Lewiston, Idaho

Page 163: Roberta and Richard Basch © Bill Lind, Still Images Portraits

Page 183: N. Scott Momaday by Lore Momaday

A NOTE ABOUT THE EDITOR

Alvin M. Josephy, Jr., was the author of many award-winning books, including *The Patriot Chiefs, The Indian Heritage of America, Now That the Buffalo's Gone, The Civil War in the American West,* and *500 Nations.* He was a vice president and editor of *American Heritage* magazine, the founding chairman of the board of trustees of the Smithsonian's National Museum of the American Indian, and president of the Western History Association. Alvin Josephy died in the fall of 2005, shortly before this book went to press.

A NOTE ON THE TYPE

The text of this book was set in Cheltenham Old Style, designed by the architect Bertram Grosvenor Goodhue in collaboration with Ingalls Kimball of the Cheltenham Press of New York. Cheltenham was introduced in the early twentieth century, a period of remarkable achievement in type design. The idea of creating a "family" of types by making variations on the basic type design was originated by Goodhue and Kimball in the design of the Cheltenham series.

COMPOSED BY
North Market Street Graphics,
Lancaster, Pennsylvania

PRINTED AND BOUND BY
Berryville Graphics, Berryville, Virginia

DESIGNED BY
Iris Weinstein

MAP BY
David Lindroth